Winning
in
Labor
Arbitration

Winning in Labor Arbitration

Walter E. Baer

740 Rush Street, Chicago, Illinois 60611

Just for Gee

Published by Crain Books
A Division of Crain Communications, Inc.
740 Rush Street
Chicago, IL 60611

84 83 82   10 9 8 7 6 5 4 3 2 1

ISBN: 0-87251-071-9
Library of Congress Number: LC 82-70973

Printed in the United States of America

Contents

v

Introduction

Arbitration is a quasi-judicial process. In essence, the purpose of arbitration is the adjudication of disputes by an impartial umpire akin to a judge in a legal action. Unlike a mediator, he does not have to suggest formulas and work out agreements. He merely hears the evidence in a dispute and hands down a decision based on the facts. Arbitrators, unlike judges in legal actions, are not bound by legal rules of evidence or by precedent.

The best arbitration is no arbitration. Yet a formal provision for arbitration—preferably, I am convinced, as the "sole and exclusive" means for final, binding decision on contract interpretation or application—is indispensable to sound contract administration. A contract that does not provide for arbitration is the labor relations equivalent of a Manx cat. Something vital is missing, without a sound evolutionary explanation for its absence.

Since World War II, labor arbitration for grievance settlement has grown rapidly. It is now provided for in 95 percent of all labor contracts in the United States. By the time parties to the labor contract resolve to go to arbitration, they are no longer interested in compromise or mutual accommodation. All such efforts have failed in previous meetings and discussions, leaving them with no recourse but to take their chances before a third party, neutral and impartial—the arbiter. Thus, when heretofore avoidable process becomes unavoidable, each party begins to worry about the "black magic" of the process and what can be done to prevail, to win. And although parties to labor agreements (but not all) today enjoy a higher level of sophistication than at any time in the past 35 years, preparation and presentation of cases to arbiters, is still too often inadequate and inept.

There is no substitute for thorough, comprehensive, detailed preparation. There is no excuse for its lack. The conscientious, dedicated, and determined advocate has learned the importance—in fact, the absolute necessity—of thorough pretrial preparation. Such an advocate probably already knows what some trial lawyers never learn, that cases are seldom if ever won in court or hearing room. They are won by the side that has slaved to find all the facts in the case and all its corporal parts and is fully prepared before any trial begins.

Preparation means giving painstaking attention to every argument, every witness, every exhibit, every precedent, every detail. It means giving equal attention to a systematic, methodical, organized, chronologically purposeful presentation—one that tells a story so logically and persuasively that the arbiter can come to only one conclusion.

Each year more of the nation's workers are being organized by unions. Each year the number of labor agreements is increasing. Each year more and more cases are referred to arbitration. And each year, thousands of individuals find themselves responsible for preparing, and then presenting, a case before the arbiter as advocates, as representatives of their companies or unions.

It is to all the current and potential practitioners in the mystical processes of arbitration that this volume is directed. Its intentions are to help each practitioner reach his goal: Winning in Arbitration.

1
Concepts—Theories—Issues

Reserved Rights in Arbitration

When the parties agree, the union usually gives up its right to strike over the issue submitted, and the employer gives up the right to take unilateral action on the matter. The employer also in effect concedes that all his decisions and actions, even those which he has previously considered properly unilateral, may eventually be subject to review by an outside party. Most employers insist, however, that they continue to have all powers they previously had until such powers have been curtailed by legislation or by an express provision of the labor agreement. This is the "reserved" or "residual" rights theory. Thus, when management spokesmen are faced with arbitration over a dispute not expressly covered by the contract, they contend the arbitrator should look to the agreement not to determine what rights they have reserved but only to determine what rights they have ceded away or agreed to share.

Such disputes most commonly appear in arbitration, for Courts seem almost eager to assign arbitrators such tasks.

One Court has said:

> When the parties have entered into a comprehensive arbitration provision, any challenge that a grievance is not intended to be covered thereunder must find support in unmistakably clear language of exclusion; arbitration of a particular dispute is to be ordered unless it may be said with positive assurance that it is excluded

1

by the contract. Whatever doubt exists as to whether the grievance is within the ambit of the arbitral process is to be resolved in favor of coverage.[1]

How have arbitrators generally viewed management's exercise of reserved rights?

Overtime—Mandatory or Optional?

Suppose the labor agreement is silent on the question of whether employee acceptance of overtime work is mandatory or optional. A typical agreement provided for time and one-half for hours over a certain number in one day and in a week, and it was considered that the provision made it "apparent that the reasonable overtime was contemplated and provisions therefore were made."[2] Another arbitrator ruled that a similar mention of overtime premium payments "clearly recognizes an obligation on the Company to pay for overtime and surely, by implication, that workers are obliged to work reasonably necessary overtime, unless specifically excused."[3]

The use of the word *normal* to describe the work day or work week has often been construed as implying that "abnormal" hours may occasionally occur. Under such clauses, arbitrators have ruled that management is not prohibited from requiring overtime work.[4] Thus we find that, absent some other contractual restriction, the performance of overtime is held to be an exclusive right of management.[5]

Job Duty Assignments and Changes

For the most part, management is allowed substantial discretion in its assignment of duties to employees. Even where there are job descriptions, Arbitrator Harold Davey held, these did not prohibit the company from adding minor duties to fill an employee's idle time.[6] Improved manufacturing processes and advanced techniques may bring about the elimination of job duties or reallocation of certain tasks. In such a case, Arbitrator Harold Gilden stated:

When, by reason of technological advancements, job content is so drastically altered as to reduce it to a mere shadow of its former dimensions, the continued survival of trivial job elements does not require the company to persist in assigning employees to that job title.[7]

Arbitrator Ralph Seward expressed a similar view in ruling that a contract did "not limit management's right to reallocate and reassign job duties in the light of technological changes."[8]

In a case with a different twist, Arbitrator Benjamin Aaron ruled that management transfer job duties from one job (the description of which mentioned the duties) to a different job classification.[9] He agreed that the Union might request reevaluation of the "receiving" job, but it could not prohibit the company from reassigning the duties. It has also been held that, in the absence of a contract clause forbidding the abolition of jobs, management is free to shift duties and consolidate jobs — so long as its action is not unreasonable or arbitrary or motivated by hostility toward the Union.[10]

When certain operations were transferred from one seniority unit to another under a silent contract, management was held to have made the transfer in the interest of efficiency where the nature of the business dictated a reasonable flexibility in assignment of work.[11]

In general, management has been given considerable latitude in making job changes, in transferring duties, and even in eliminating tasks and jobs.

Establishing Plant Rules

Management's right to make and enforce plant rules to preserve the health, welfare, and safety of its employees has also been well established.[12]

Arbitrator Dudley Whiting has stated that, "In the absence of any contractual limitation, an employer has a complete right to direct the activities of its employees by establishing and enforcing rules of conduct."[13] Arbitrator Vernon Stouffer has expressed a similar view that "Such rules, so long as they are reasonable, need not be negotiated and it is a reserved right and prerogative of management to establish such rules."[14]

Although arbitrators usually affirm the right of management to promulgate and enforce reasonable rules of conduct which are essential to efficient functioning of its plant, they support, on the other hand, the right of employees to challenge management's application of such rules; they will uphold the employee's complaint if the employer has been unfair, arbitrary, or discriminatory.[15]

In the absence of any contractual requirement, arbitrators have held that the company may not be required to post written rules and penalties, since that determination is part of the managerial function of directing the work force.[16] However, employees cannot be expected to comply with certain standards of conduct and behavior unless such rules are communicated to them.[17]

Withdrawal and Return to Bargaining Unit

Under silent contracts, decisions vary as to whether employees who have transferred out of the unit may return to the unit with seniority intact.

Where the union contended that unit employees accepting supervisory positions forfeited seniority, an arbitrator ruled that the employees should be allowed to retain the seniority accumulated prior to their promotion, but not accumulate any while serving as supervisors.[18] Arbitrator Ronald Haughton, in a similar dispute, allowed the employee to accumulate seniority during a temporary period of promotion outside of the unit.[19]

Where employees had transferred from one bargaining unit into a different bargaining unit, Arbitrator Harry Platt decided that the contract did not permit these employees to retain seniority since this would have given them "an underserved windfall in that they would have seniority rights simultaneously in two different contract units."[20] The employees involved were considered as voluntary terminations from their original unit.

Subcontracting

Arbitration awards pursuant to management subcontracting under silent agreements appear to float in a twilight zone. Some arbitrators have found implied restrictions on this management right in the recognition clause,[21] the seniority clause,[22] and the job classification listing.[23]

Most authorities, however, refuse to imply restrictions and adopt, instead, the reserved rights concept, while imposing certain standards for evaluating the propriety of the subcontracting. Factors which singly or in combination have been decisive in such cases include the effect of the action on the union,[24] the availability of qualified employees,[25] the availability of facilities and equipment,[26] the duration and regularity of the subcontracting,[27] past practice,[28] negotiation history,[29] the effect on the unit,[30] and the type of work performed.[31]

Conclusions

These are merely a sampling of the disputes which can arise under silent agreements. Most managements attempt to reinforce their position through carefully constructed management rights clauses; in their definition of a grievance; in their limitations on the arbitrator's purview and in strict avoidance of mutual-consent and joint-committee clauses.

Grievance and Arbitration Provisions

By their almost universal use of the grievance and arbitration clauses in collective bargaining, labor and management have clearly evidenced a willingness to forego economic warfare and instead cooperate to settle controversies arising out of contracts.

Almost all major agreements providing for a grievance procedure also provide for final and binding arbitration of grievance disputes. This widespread reliance upon voluntary arbitration to resolve grievance disputes is characteristic of the American system of collective bargaining and unparalleled among other industrialized countries. Thousands of disputes are arbitrated in the United States each year under these procedures; even in companies in which no disputes reach the stage of arbitration, the availability of the procedure undoubtedly exercises a stabilizing influence.

When the earlier steps of the procedure work satisfactorily, arbitrators are at best fifth wheels and at worst "bogey men" standing just outside the scene and thereby inducing the parties to make their own solutions. It is only when the machinery at the earlier steps doesn't work well that they are called in. The percentage of grievances settled without arbitration certainly exceeds 90 percent. In many plants the arbitration procedure has never been used. The system simply provides a safety valve, allowing steam to escape from industrial pressure cookers.

The parties themselves customarily place some general restrictions upon the arbiter. Such restraints appear in more than three-fifths of all arbitration provisions. Most of these (88 percent) provide that the arbiter may not alter or add to the terms or intent of the contract; more than 20 percent specifically rule out arbitration of general wage issues; about 8 percent specifically exclude production standards (this exclusion is particularly common in the automobile industry), and 2 percent forbid inclusion of safety and health issues (half of these are in the contracts of transportation equipment companies).

Most agreements limit retroactivity of arbitral remedy to the date the grievance was first presented in writing.

Let's analyze a typical arbitration provision. This is not represented to be an ideal or perfect clause—there are none.

Article VIII—Grievance Procedure and Arbitration

Section 1 – A grievance is any dispute or complaint of employees arising from or based on a violation of this Agreement by the Company. Any disputes, complaints, or grievances arising from alleged violations of this agreement by the Company shall be settled and determined through the following procedure:

Step (a) — Any employee having a grievance will first attempt to settle same with his immediate supervisor, it being understood that the employee shall have the right to request that a Steward be present at this step of the grievance procedure, and it being further understood and agreed that the disposition of grievances at this step of the grievance procedure shall not constitute a precedent for the interpretation and administration of this Agreement.

Step (b) — If a grievance is not settled at Step (1) of the grievance procedure, it shall then be reduced to writing, and the aggrieved employee, the Steward, and the Company's administrator will then attempt to settle the grievance.

Step (c) — If a grievance is not settled at Step (b) of the grievance procedure, the Company's Administrator or other official of the Company (together with such associates as he may wish to assist him in the matter) and an officer of the Union (together with such associates as he may wish to assist him in the matter) shall then attempt to settle the grievance, and the Company shall thereafter give the Union its answer to said grievance in writing.

Step (d) — If the grievance is not then satisfactorily settled and if the grievance is otherwise arbitrable under this Agreement, it may be referred to arbitration in strict accordance with the provisions of this Agreement pertaining to arbitration, but not otherwise, provided, however, that if the Union fails to notify the Company in writing by registered United States mail within 10 days after the Company gives its answer in writing to a grievance (Step (c) of the grievance procedure above), then the Union shall be conclusively presumed to have accepted the Company's answer thereto and said grievance shall not thereafter be arbitrable.

Section 2 – Any disputes, complaints, or grievances arising from alleged violations of this Agreement by the Company shall be deemed, considered, and held to have been waived unless the same are presented for settlement and determination at Step (a) of the grievance procedure of this Agreement within 2 work days from the date on which said dispute, complaint or grievance first arose. The Union shall have 5 work days from the date on which the Company gives its answer at Steps (a) and (b), respectively, to appeal a grievance from Step (a) to Step (b) and from Step (b) to Step (c) of this grievance procedure.

Section 3 – The Company shall not be required or obligated under the terms of this Agreement or otherwise to submit to arbitration any claim or cause of action which it may have or assert on account of any alleged violation of this Agreement by the Union or any employees covered by this Agreement. The Company shall have the right to sue at law or in equity in any court of competent jurisdiction, Federal or State, to enforce this Agreement and to recover for any breach or violation thereof.

Section 4 – No grievance shall be arbitrable unless it involves an alleged material violation by the Company of one or more specific provisions of this Agreement, which alleged violation shall be designated in writing by the Union to the Company no later than the time such grievance is appealed to Step (b) of the grievance procedure hereinbefore set forth. No grievance shall be arbitrable if it is frivolous, or it is nonarbitrable under the "Management Prerogatives" Article of this Agreement.

Strict compliance with the procedural requirements and time limits of the foregoing grievance procedure is a condition precedent to the Union's right to take any grievance to arbitration; it being understood and agreed, however, that any of said time limits may be extended by mutual agreement in writing between the Company and the Union. In the absence of such compliance, the grievance shall be deemed to have been waived and shall not be arbitrable under this Article. No arbitrator shall have authority to determine questions of compliance with these procedural requirements and time limits, unless such questions are specifically submitted to an arbitrator by express agreement of both parties.

No grievance may be filed or considered which is based on an occurrence preceding the date of this Agreement. No arbitrator may make an award of reinstatement or back pay, or any other award, with respect to any period after the expiration of this Agreement.

Section 5 – In any case where the Company claims that an alleged grievance is not arbitrable because a function or prerogative of management is involved or questioned, or where the Company claims that the grievance sought to be arbitrated is not arbitrable because it is frivolous or does not involve an alleged material violation by the Company of one or more specific provisions of this agreement, or is foreclosed from arbitration by reason of any provision of Section 4 of this Article VIII, and gives the Union its reasons in writing for such claim, it shall not be a violation of this Agreement for the Company to refuse to arbitrate such grievance unless and until a final judicial determination has been made in a suit under Section 301 of the Labor Management Relations Act, 1947, as amended, or other appropriate legal action, that said grievance is arbitrable under the terms of this Agreement, provided, however, the Court first decides that the Company's refusal to arbitrate such grievance was arbitrary and unreasonable.

Section 6 – Any grievance which is otherwise arbitrable under the terms of this Agreement shall be arbitrated in accordance with the rules of the American Arbitration Association which are then in effect and the Arbitrator for each such case shall be selected in accordance with said rules. The Arbitrator so selected shall have power to receive relevant testimony from the parties to the dispute and to hear such witnesses as they may desire to present. The parties may, if they so desire, be represented by counsel in all proceedings had before the Arbitrator. At the request of either party, the Arbitrator shall hold a prehearing conference for the purpose of defining, simplifying and framing the issue or issues to be arbitrated, and ascertaining the positions of the respective parties concerning said issues. The Company shall bear the cost of preparing and presenting its case to the Arbitrator and the Union shall bear the cost of preparing and presenting its case to the Arbitrator. All other expenses of arbitration, such as, but not limited to, the Arbitrator's fee, the cost of recording and transcribing testimony, and the hiring of a space in which the arbitration proceedings are held, shall be divided equally between the Company and the Union.

Section 7 – The function of the Arbitrator shall be of a judicial rather than a legislative nature. The Arbitrator shall not have the authority to add to, ignore, or modify any of the terms or provisions of this Agreement. The Arbitrator shall never in any degree or to any extent substitute his judgment for the Company's judgment, and where matters of judgment are involved (if the case is otherwise arbitrable under this Agreement) he shall be limited to deciding whether or not the Company acted capriciously or in bad faith. The Arbitrator shall not decide issues which are not directly involved in the case submitted to him, and no decision of the Arbitrator shall require the payment of a wage rate or wage basis different from, or the payment of any wages in addition to, those expressly set forth in this agreement. Subject to the foregoing qualifications and limitations, the Arbitrator's award shall be final and binding upon the Company, the Union, and the aggrieved employee or employees.

Section 8 – Only the Union shall have the right to prosecute grievances under this Agreement and only the Union shall have the right to take to arbitration any grievance which is otherwise arbitrable under this Agreement. If the Union fails, refuses, or declines to

> prosecute a grievance on behalf of an employee, or if the Company and the Union settle any grievance on behalf of an employee hereunder, the employee who has filed such grievance or on whose behalf it has been filed shall be conclusively bound thereby and both the Union and the aggrieved employee shall thereafter be estopped to revive or further prosecute said grievance.

This clause contains most of the elements customarily found in such clauses—plus some special ingredients.

First, it contains time limits for the raising, filing, and processing of alleged grievances. It also contains penalties for exceeding the contractual time limitations.

Experience having shown that disputes are easier resolved when promptly dealt with, most parties to labor contracts view such clauses as desirable. Allowing grievances to grow stale further irritates an employee already sufficiently dissatisfied to bring a grievance. Without time limits to keep them moving along, grievances also tend to bunch up, clogging the procedure and angering employees impatient for some solution, or a mere response, to their complaint.

However, time limitation provisions also contain the seeds of other problems. An employee may inadvertently fail to raise a complaint within the contract's unyielding time periods. Union officials may also err. In a contractual grievance procedure with a strict 2-day time limit, for example, the third day might as well be the ninth, or the ninetieth; the contract is just as unforgiving. Technically the dispute is no longer a viable proposition. But for the involved employee, the matter is still very much alive, and unresolved. If he has been discharged, the rightness or wrongness of termination will now never be judged. If he has been improperly laid off, or paid incorrectly, or wrongly denied the benefit of some contract provision, the injustice will never be corrected.

Under the contract example above certain matters are not arbitrable at all; the parties involved, the Company and the Union, consider this to be in their very best self-interest.

If the matter in dispute was not bargained for and contractually committed to, it isn't within the entitlement of the Union and the employees and should not be arbitrable.

Experience in administration of contracts has produced problematical situations which have steered the parties toward such clauses to safeguards of their interests. This is quite natural and understandable. The relationship between Company and Union is basically a business relationship with each having its own peculiar needs, problems, and objectives—some of which may put one party in conflict with the other. The labor contract is a legal document which binds that business relationship together and spells out its terms and conditions, its breadth and scope.

But an employee who believes he has a complaint rarely is legally trained. As a matter of fact, he often is not familiar with the provisions of the labor contract which covers him; he may never even have seen a copy of it. In fact, the contract clauses were designed primarily to meet and protect the interest of the institutions, not the people employed.

Therefore, the very provisions which best serve the parties who agreed to them may not serve the best interests of employees governed by them—at least in the view of those employees. And the attitudes, opinions, and reactions of the employees too often lead them into conduct which is in breach of the contract.

Precedent Value of Arbitration Awards

How do prior arbitration awards relate to current controversies, under the same, a succeeding, or a different contract, and before the same or a different arbitrator? Is an arbitrator, like a court, bound to consider earlier disputes and the decisions of other tribunals? This question has been the source of continuing argument for many years; the very nature of the arbitration process, as it exists today, conceals from its own disciples a definite, specific answer.

It appears that the great majority of arbitrators are willing to give only "some weight" to prior awards. But what do arbitrators consider to be "some weight?"[32]

It seems to be an established principle in the arbitration process that arbitration opinions are not precedents—that each case stands upon its own feet. However, it also appears to be well-established that interpretations of contract language embodied in an award become a part of that contract language. This doctrine is not seriously threatened even by those who protest against "citations" and "precedent." As a matter of industrial reality, a decision is "precedent" until the parties change its effect in the labor agreement or another arbitrator changes or confuses it with a contrary ruling.

Arbitrators, moreover, seldom give much notice to the legal differences among various types of precedents. Res adjudicata is the universally recognized judicial doctrine which forbids retrial of matters which have been previously settled by a binding decision. The rule rests upon considerations of judicial time and public policy (factors not necessarily present in private arbitration hearings) favoring the establishment of certainty in legal relations. The judgment of the court puts a practical end to the dispute so that none of the issues included or includable can be brought again into litigation between the parties upon any ground whatever, in the absence of fraud or some other overwhelming factor which would operate to invalidate the judgment.[33]

Not so in arbitration!

Arbitrators' awards are not accorded this weight of "judicial authority" in determining future controversies, even between the same parties or over the same issues. In arbitration, all questions of fact and law are deemed to be referred to the arbitrator for decision. Unless restricted by the contract, or submission agreement, or state statute, arbitrators do not bind themselves by strict rules of law or evidence. The arbitrator is free to decide the issues submitted to him, notwithstanding any prior awards between the parties, unless the parties have agreed otherwise.

What then is "some weight?"

An examination of a large number of reported cases reveals that prior awards often do play a part in arbitration. But rather than carrying the weight of "judicial authority," they exert a "persuasive" force. The extent to which this persuasive force is in fact compelling in a given case is generally influenced by such factors as:

(1) Is the present fact situation the same as the prior fact situation?

(2) Are the same two parties involved?

(3) Is the language of the labor agreement identical in both cases?

(4) If the same parties and the same labor agreement are involved, has a contract negotiation occurred in the meantime, and if so, were the contractual provisions changed?

(5) Subsequent to the first award, has a practice come into existence, mutually agreeable to the parties, which has the effect of modifying all or part of the prior award?[34]

(6) Has another award been rendered which reverses or contradicts the prior award?

(7) Is there new evidence and argument being presented which was not considered in the prior case?

(8) Did the prior award enunciate just and reasonable principles of conduct and contract interpretation?

> A frequent problem for arbitrators occurs when a party to an arbitration cites other published cases, presumably identical or very nearly so with the present case, which upon close examination prove to be dissimilar or unrelated.[35] Naturally, the parties do not enhance the in any case questionable value of cited cases when they do not exercise extreme care in research and selection.

Reference to such elusive precedent reminds one of the story told by Erick Heller in which a clown appears on a stage completely darkened except for a small circle of light cast by a street lamp in one corner. The clown, his face deeply worried and long-drawn, walks round and round this circle of light, obviously desperately looking for something.

> "What have you lost?" asks a policeman passing by.
>
> "The key to my house!"
>
> Whereupon the policeman joins in the search. Finding nothing after a while, the policeman inquires, "Are you certain you lost it here?"
>
> "No," replies the clown, and pointing to the dark corner of the stage, says, "Over there."
>
> "Then why are you looking for it over here?"
>
> "Because there is no light over there," replies the clown.[36]

Obviously, if the parties carry any hope for the arbitrator to find their precedential key, they must first have him looking in lighted places.

However, when a cited case does strike on all fours, an arbitrator may apply its reasoning to his case. Referring to a union cited case, Arbitrator B. Meredith Reid stated:

> With the reasoning there, as far as it went, your arbitrator agrees and uses its principles to state this Board finds it a fact and thus overrules that portion of the company's position which claimed the grievants herein were 'temporary employees'; they were not.[37]

The relevance of prior awards, obtained in disputes decided between the same parties, is also affected by similarities in the fact situations. For instance, an arbitrator in a prior case had ordered a company to pay call-out pay to an electrician because a kiln operator had changed a light bulb. In a later case, Arbitrator LeRoy Autrey denied a claim by another electrician for call-out pay because a maintenance mechanic had changed a light bulb: the kiln operator had not been authorized to handle electrical equipment, but the maintenance mechanic was. Autrey disregarded the prior award because the bulb change did not require any high degree of skill, nor did it present any safety hazards.[38]

Where the previous decision appears reasonable after a fair hearing, arbitrators are cautious about rendering a different solution.[39] Carrying this principle another step forward, Arbitrator Whitley P. McCoy came upon a situation in which he considered prior awards to have precedent value. McCoy stated:

> Where a number of competing companies negotiate jointly with a union, and agree on identical contract provisions in order to avoid competitive disadvantages, it would seem that the mutual intent of the several parties would be nullified if arbitrators should, by contradictory interpretations of identical language, destroy the identity of meaning.[40]

He ruled that a decision by one arbitrator under these circumstances should be followed by another unless it is clearly wrong; finding that an earlier award had held salaried personnel entitled to a full forty hours salary for any week in which they worked at all under this contract, he made the same ruling.

Despite their protestations to the contrary, arbitrators have been known to "go along" with prior awards, even those to which they do not wholly subscribe, thus giving them persuasive precedent value—for the sake of stability and certainty between the parties in their contract interpretations. Jacob Seidenberg, Chairman of a Special Board of Adjustment, expressing the opinion that had the case been before him for the first time he might have decided otherwise, nevertheless ruled that a pay dispute had to be resolved in accord with prior awards on the same subject involving the same agreement.[41] In a similar case of greater complexity and wider ranging implications, Arbitrator Robert W. Fleming decided it was not important whether he might have decided a prior case differently. Although the dispute before him was between another plant and another local of the union, Fleming followed previous awards under the same National Agreement and denied the grievance.[42]

Arbitrators will reverse a fellow arbiter when they feel

he has erroneously interpreted a contract clause.[43] However, such reversals appear to be a minority exception to the general rule of following "good sense" prior rulings.

Although arbitrators usually minimize the importance of the precedent value of other awards, they do find sufficient merit in them to research how other arbitrators have ruled in similar cases.[44] They may even invite and encourage the parties to submit citations.[45]

Obviously if one party or the other finds a particular award so objectionable as to be motivated to change the contract language, and succeeds in doing so in collective bargaining negotiations, the same case brought a second time under changed language may understandably bring a different ruling, even before the same arbitrator. However, the language change must be "sufficient to change the meaning." In an International Harvester case, an arbiter found that the contract language change purportedly accomplished to reverse the rule established by a prior award was in the final analysis insufficient to change the meaning of the earlier clause.[46]

Arbitrators are also fairly consistent in giving substantial weight to prior awards where negotiation has occurred since the previous ruling, and the contractual language has not been changed. This was emphasized by Arbitrator Peter Seitz:

> The Impartial Chairman is aware that the conflicting views as to whether the Turkus Award applied to the handling of comics and rotos for suburban wholesalers and news companies were known to each of the parties at the time they were engaged in negotiations looking to the execution of a new Agreement. This conflict was not resolved in the negotiations. The Impartial Chairman is not disposed to regard the failure to do so as evidence of what the parties agreed to for the new contract term—but he is obliged to take this circumstance into consideration in determining what weight and effect to give to the Turkus Award. *When they went into negotiations they both knew that an arbitration award had been issued establishing a rule,* at

the very minimum, affecting operations and overtime pay for direct delivery. Inasmuch as the same employees and crews in the same premises handle rotos and comics for both direct and indirect deliveries, *the union was on notice that unless the Turkus Award (whatever its scope) were changed by negotiations, in any subsequently held arbitration hearing involving the inextricably enmeshed operations for the handling of materials destined for indirect delivery, that Turkus Award, necessarily would be given precedential weight* [47] (emphasis supplied).

Obviously the possibility of conflict between decisions of arbitrators is one of the risks of the arbitral process. It is partly to minimize this danger that parties sometimes enter into contractual arrangements for permanent rather than ad hoc arbitrators. Naturally, under a permanent arbitration system, the likelihood of conflicts between decisions is greatly lessened.

An excellent example of the difference between the two systems is the Chrysler-UAW permanent umpire arrangement:

In every case the chairman makes a careful review of all previous decisions that are indicated to be relevant to the matter at hand. Often his findings are rested in whole or in part on the principles enunciated in the earlier cases. Frequently, patterns and standards are evolved gradually on a case by case basis, with determinations being made on various aspects of a particular problem. Contract provisions once construed are uniformly applied, until such time as the parties themselves may see fit to negotiate changes. Consistency of principles and their application is sought, not for its own sake but as a matter of fairness and as an aid to promoting predictability at the arbitration step and workability in the parties' collective bargaining relationships. In this manner, a body of case law is built up, and the system becomes institutionalized.

The parties themselves recognize the precedent value of the decisions, not only in arbitration cases, but also in their day-to-day relationships. Although only two copies of a decision are issued to each side, both parties reproduce copies in large quantities and distribute them widely among officials and representatives of their organizations. For ready reference, they supplement this by maintaining their own indexes and digests of cases. At the local levels, the parties attempt to make plant practices conform to principles announced in umpire decisions. There, they refer to decided cases in the working out of problems at the pre-grievance stage, or in the early steps of the grievance procedure. At the top levels, the decisions are almost always given immediate application in analogous disputes which may be, or come, before the (four-man) appeal board.[48]

In summary, the following of precedent in the usual ad hoc arbitration process rests primarily upon the assumption that the precedent has continuing validity. But where a conflict in decisions results from a clear and supported conviction that the earlier decision does not reasonably resolve the issue, an arbitrator need not abdicate to his predecessor that function of judgment for which he was engaged.[49]

Although the doctrine of "stare decisis, et non quieta movere" (adhere to precedents, do not unsettle things) does not strictly apply to arbitration, nevertheless, the value of the predictability of decisions to parties in the contractual relationship and the reluctance to unsettle matters previously established are desirable elements in arbitration. Obviously, a primary purpose of the arbitral system is to help the parties reach a clear understanding of the meaning of their agreement as applied in the plant. Relitigation of decided issues, repeated attempts to persuade an arbitrator to change an established contract interpretation merely because one side or the other does not like it, and refusal to accept arbitral decisions as the basis for settling disputes without arbitration cannot fail to defeat this purpose.

Arbitrators can also make a positive contribution by laying a heavy burden of proof and persuasion on the party that claims a prior award was erroneous and should be reversed. The burden must clearly be heaviest in cases involving the same contractual provision as the prior case, the same facts, the same parties, and no new evidence or argument. Here prior awards must be accorded persuasive value in the interest of stability to the decisional process.

Subcontracting—Twilight Zone in the Management Function

What is subcontracting? Many people become emotionally involved, the mere utterance of the word causing the pulse to throb, the adrenal gland to secrete, and the temperature to rise dangerously. The ironic point is that the reaction is the same for representatives of both union and management. When rational, how do these same people define it?

In its broadest sence, subcontracting means arranging with another firm to make goods or perform services which could be performed by bargaining unit employees with the company's facilities.

Since the definition is so simple, why does the word generate so much heat?

There is no question that an entire book could be devoted to the views of the National Labor Relations Board on management's actions in contracting out. A second book could then be written on the rulings of the courts and their impact upon subcontracting. But although the parties to labor agreements much too often find themselves in these arenas, the tribunal they frequent is that of arbitration.

Contracts with express provisions on contracting out generally either limit management's prerogatives, in whole or in part, or expressly provide management with an un-hindered right.[50] Therefore, I am limiting my attention to the more elusive subject of implied limitations[51] and how arbitrators wrestle with this issue.

Arbitrators and Implied Restrictions
Where the contract contains no explicit language to bar subcontracting, arbitrators usually turn to particular clauses to find some implied intention to limit contracting out.

The provisions most frequently referred to, singly or in combination, are: the recognition clause, the seniority clause, the list of job classifications, and related clauses.

The recognition clause is merely the statement in the labor agreement that the employer recognizes a particular union as the exclusive bargaining agent of employees in the appropriate unit. However, many unions and some arbitrators have said that this clause implies an agreement that the employer may not, by managerial decision, remove work from employees in the unit by subcontracting it to others. This theory was articulated by Arbitrator C. R. Schedler:

> There is no express language either prohibiting or authorizing contracting out. *What is more important* is that *the contract contains a clause recognizing the Union* —the infraction here is in the unavoidable effect on these rights. To me it is clear that the work belonged to the unit which contained employees fully capable of executing it. The contracting out had the inevitable impact of derogating the Union's status as recognized exclusive representative.[52] (emphasis supplied)

Arbitrators who employ this clause as a source of work jurisdiction fail to recognize that the National Labor Relations Act requires recognition of the union as the representative of people—not work.

Perhaps the most complete answer to those who seek to find an implied agreement or limitation in the recognition clause was given by Professor Herman Gray of New York University, who stated in Hearst Consolidated Publications:

> In my view, the purpose of the Recognition Clause is no more than to enunciate the legal status of the bargaining union. It describes the unit of the employees for whom the Union speaks and thus delineates the operative scope of the agreement itself. It serves no substantive function. That is, it does not deal with and has no bearing upon the terms and conditions governing the employment itself. To read substantive provisions into the Recognition Clause through arbitration

decisions is, in my judgment, to use arbitration as a means for expanding the agreement which the parties have made, rather than just interpreting and applying its provisions in specific situations.[53]

It is the recognition clause which most frequently captures the fancy of arbitrators who search for implied limitations on contracting out.

The seniority clause presumably establishes a simple preference for longer-service employees over shorter-service employees when work is made available by the employer. Since such clauses provide that the shorter-service employees will be laid off first, it obviously recognizes that the volume of work can diminish.[54]

However, Arbitrator Saul Wallen rejected a Managements Rights Clause in favor of seniority provisions of the labor agreement in New Britain Machine:

> Job security is an inherent element of the labor contract, a part of its very being. If wages is the heart of the labor agreement, job security may be considered its soul. Those eligible to share in the degree of job security the contract affords are those to whom the contract applies.... The transfer of work customarily performed by employees in the bargaining unit must therefore be regarded as an attack on the job security of the employees whom the agreement covers and therefore on one of the contract's basic purposes.[55]

Arbitrators, being only human, sometimes change their minds. Ten years later, Arbitrator Wallen had this to say in Hershey Chocolate Corporation:

> In the same way the seniority provisions guarantee, not a constant employment opportunity for each category of employee covered by the contract, but a set of rules for the parcelling out of employment opportunities, the availability of work can be affected by diminished work volumes due to changes in the market, due to changes in technology, or due to changes in the realm of good faith managerial decision-making.[56]

Reasonableness and Good Faith Standards

What about arbitrators who refuse to imply restrictions? Basically, they seem to hold the view that management has reserved the right to contract out, unless this right has been limited by specific contract language. But they do impose a certain standard to evaluate the propriety of the subcontract action.[57] The standards below are factors which singly, or in combination, have been decisive in certain cases:

a. *The effect on the Union:* Was the subcontracting done to injure or discriminate against the Union? Did it substantially prejudice the status of the unit?[58]

b. *The availability of qualified employees:* Did members of the unit possess skills adequate to perform the required work and were such employees readily available in the numbers needed?[59]

c. *The availability of facilities and equipment:* Were equipment and facilities currently or readily available at reasonable cost?[60]

d. *The duration and regularity:* Was the contracting out temporary or permanent? Was it done frequently or only occasionally?[61]

e. *Negotiation history:* Had the subject been discussed in negotiations?[62]

f. *Past practice:* Had work been contracted out in the past? To what extent?[63]

In the union's quest for greater job security, management assignment of work must be a principal target. And that's where the second pincer's claw—arbitration—is used as the instrument to attack managements' unilateral decisions.

The Supreme Court dealt a body blow to the reserved rights theory by its holding that "everything management does is subject to the agreement when it contains arbitration." The Court has also said that, where arbitration is provided for in a contract, "only the most forceful evidence of a purpose to exclude" a given type of claim will keep it out of arbitration.

Past Practice and Custom

Investigation of the many published decisions involving past practice makes it clear that arbitrators are far from unanimous about precise standards of application. The decision in any particular case appears to depend greatly upon the individual thinking of the particular arbitrator deciding the issue. Archibald Cox once stated:

> Outside the areas controlled by statute, there is no more important treasury of experience than the record of grievance arbitration. Surely arbitrators have not labored at the administration of collective bargaining agreements for almost two decades without arriving at some generalization upon which the unbiased can agree, even though partisan interests preclude unanimity.[64]

It is true that many practitioners representing both labor and management have found some guiding generalizations in arbitral opinion which have provided predictable outcomes on certain issues. Past practice does not appear to be one of those issues. Here there are at best only uncertain generalizations.

But it is still necessary to attempt to provide some idea of the type of standards generally applied by arbitrators. I believe that the majority of arbitration decisions where past practice or custom was given some influential weight in the final outcome contained one or more of the following four ingredients. Conversely, where the party pressing for compelling consideration of past practice failed to establish that one or more of these same ingredients existed, the award went to the other party. The past practice must have been:

(1) *Unequivocal:* The practice has been applied consistently, uniformly, regularly, and without break.

(2) *Clearly Enunciated:* The practice has been acquiesced in by the parties and has operated without protest or objection from one party or the other.

(3) *Of Long Standing:* It has been followed over a reasonably long period of time. In this regard, some arbitrators may be influenced by the bridge effect resulting when a practice commencing under one agreement continues unchanged and unprotested into a renewed agreement, bridging the collective bargaining negotiations. The frequency of the practice may not be as consequential as the consistency of its application. In other words, a practice applied consistently only three times a year may conceivably have more weight than another practice applied fifteen times a year, but inconsistently.

(4) *Jointly Accepted and Acted Upon:* Both parties through their line representatives have operated as though the practice was a guiding rule. This may signify to some arbitrators a mutuality which implies that the practice results from bilateral action as opposed to unilateral action.

Arbitrator Whitley P. McCoy, serving as chairman of a tripartite board for Kaiser Aluminum and Chemical Corporation and the Aluminum Workers International Union, ruled in favor of a binding past practice in a call-in pay dispute. Employees who had completed their regular 8:00 A.M. to 4:00 P.M. shift on one day and were then called and told to report early on the following day, were not entitled to four hours pay for time worked prior to 8:00 A.M. on the second day, even though the contract provided (1) that the work day was from 8:00 A.M. to 8:00 A.M. and (2) that employees called in to work on the second shift within the same work day should be paid for not less than four hours' work.

Three features—(1) uniformity, (2) acquiescence by the parties, and (3) long continued practice—all influenced the decision.

The company proved that a uniform practice has existed, where the man called out has continued to work on into his regular shift, to count the time on his regular shift in computing the minimum of four hours paid for. An employee of the company's payroll department testified that so far as he knew payment had always been made as it was made in this case, when a man called out continued working into his regular shift. He testified that he had made a random check and had been unable to find any instance of paying allowed time under the circumstances. Other supervisors testified as to instances that they recalled where payment had been made in the same manner as in this case. They testified as to these instances, giving names and circumstances. The union offered no evidence of an instance where payment had been made in accordance with its interpretation of this contract section.

Uniform and long-continued practice, known to and concurred in by both parties, is of course good evidence as to the intent placed upon contract language by the parties.[65]

A practice that was consistent though relatively infrequent was considered compelling in a dispute resolved by Hubert C. Callaghan for the North American Cement Corporation and the United Cement, Lime, and Gypsum Workers union. The arbiter ruled that four instances in eight and one-half years were sufficient to establish a practice of filling job vacancies by lottery when two of four applicants for the vacancy had equal seniority and the minimum ability required for the job. Another element, that of acquiescence, was evident since the union had not previously protested. The arbiter asked himself: In labor relations, how many instances are necessary to establish a practice? The answer varies with the situation. If the problem normally occurs fairly frequently, and is not dealt with in the contract, a relatively large number of instances might be required to establish a practice. But if the problem occurs rarely, as in the case before the arbiter, a relatively small number of instances might be sufficient to establish a practice.[66]

The bridge effect, length of practice, and acquiescence were principal ingredients in a dispute resolved by Harold

M. Gilden. Despite the fact that a retirement plan was established unilaterally, compulsory retirement of employees at an age fixed by plan was ruled proper, since the retirement plan had been in effect for a long period of time and the union had not previously protested:

> In this issue, the union is attempting to do by means of arbitration what it could not accomplish during negotiations. It bargained with full knowledge of the company's retirement policy and accepted the language which appears in the local agreements. The union, by its silence, either has abandoned its objections to the retirement program, or at least yielded to an established management prerogative.

> This is not a situation where the company is attempting to inaugurate a retirement policy. The arbitrator is here presented with a tenuous claim based on an unrealistic and startling definition of the word "discharge." He is being asked to rewrite a contract agreed to by the parties in the light of years of past practice and interpretation, and to throw open to dispute the resulting multitude of thorny problems.[67]

Edgar A. Jones also endorsed the bridge concept:

> It is well accepted that a course of conduct engaged in by one party and acquiesced in by the other party to a collective bargaining agreement, spanning two or more contract terms—without any interim contractual reaction to it—becomes a part of the agreement between the parties and cannot be substantially altered or discontinued except by bilateral negotiations.[68]

Arbitrator McCoy agreed:

> The contract does not contain any provision concerning this matter. However, it could hardly be denied that plant practices and customs have existed at the time the contract was executed, bearing on working conditions and which the parties did not contemplate changing, are by implication a part of the contract.[69]

Past practice was clearly controlling in a case where the bridge effect, acquiescence by the union without protest, and long and consistent administration were compelling. The contract granted vacation pay at the employee's regular rate, defined as the employee's straight time rate on the job to which he was regularly assigned at the time of becoming eligible for vacation. The aggrieved employee had been transferred to a lower rated job one week before vacation and vacation pay was computed at the lower rate, since the company's practice for many years had been to pay for vacations at the same rate the employee would have received if he had actually been at work. There was no evidence that the method of computation had been deliberately chosen to give an employee less vacation pay than he was entitled to receive. Arbitrator Joseph M. Klamon said:

> It is a universally recognized rule that in interpreting a contract clause capable of more than one meaning, the intention of the parties as evidenced in long established past practice is an important and often a controlling factor.... When a method of computing vacation pay is not challenged either in grievance procedure or during contract negotiations for many years of collective bargaining history, it is reasonable to find and to hold as we do that the past practice of the company in computing such vacation pay on the basis that it has used for many years has met with at least the implied assent of the union.... If the parties wish to effect a drastic change, or spell out more specifically a different interpretation than the one clearly established and accepted by the union without protest over many years of past practice, they can only do so during the next contract negotiations or by supplemental agreement to the present contract.[70]

The case is interesting also because it discloses one of the avenues open to any party which has become encumbered by a practice undesirable to them. In this case the union would be waiting until the agreement expired to accomplish this objective, since the company was probably satisfied with the outcome. However, the union might be able to persuade the employer to engage in negotiations on this subject during the term of the agreement, provided it was ready to grant a concession of greater consequence to the employer than the vacation decision.

Arbitrator Paul Prasow found the duration of a practice and the union's acquiescence to it to be controlling in a Proctor and Gamble case. The classification of packer was one which under the contract was confined to female employees, and in its performance, jar unpacking was inherently related to, and an integral part of, the packing line. The union contended that unpacking, as contrasted to packing, was unsuitable for women and that jar unpackers were not included in the contract listing of women's jobs. The governing factor was past practice. For over two years, there was an acceptance by the union of the company's interpretation that jar unpacker was a woman's job. Where the relations of the parties through their previous dealings or through other circumstances are such as to impose a duty to speak, silence on the part of the union over the two-year period could conceivably, in management's mind, constitute acceptance of this interpretation.[71] Moreover the union had not raised the issue in negotiations on the new contract, even during specific bargaining discussions regarding packing lines in the factory.

Another employer did not have the right, without the consent of the union, to discontinue its practice of granting leaves of absence to pregnant employees and to adopt instead a policy requiring discharge when work deteriorated or risk of injury became evident. An employee who had been discharged under this new policy was reinstated with back pay from the time of her discharge except for a five-week period during which she would have been absent on leave. The evidence made it clear that maternity leaves were a long-established, important, and known pracice, though not specifically referred to in the contract. The practice had thus ripened into an integral part of the bargaining relationship and became a condition of employment which the employees and the union understandably had a reasonable expectation would continue.[72]

The scheduling of lunch periods and the impact of past practice upon management's right to change them was the question presented to Arbitrator Clarence M. Updegraff by the Bake-Lite Company and the United Glass and Ceramic Workers Union. On the shift of work which ran from 8:00 A.M. to 4:00 P.M. , the practice had been to schedule lunch periods in four 30-minute periods between 11:00 A.M. and 1:00 P.M. The employer unilaterally changed the schedule of lunch periods to five 30-minute periods between 10:45 A.M. and 1:15 P.M. The text of the agreement contained nothing about the time for lunch periods of shift workers. The union felt that the change in schedule placed the earliest and latest lunch periods unreasonably near the beginning and end of the shift, causing some to work two hours and 45 minutes before lunch and then four hours and 45 minutes after lunch, and vice versa. The union was also concerned about even further extensions. The arbitrator felt that past practice had been so uniform that the time for luncheon periods had to be regarded as restricted to the two-hour period from 11:00 A.M. to 1:00 P.M.[73] Here again all four ingredients were instrumental in the result.

Arbitrator Paul M. Hebert clearly stated his complete agreement with the various principles under discussion here:

> Past practice to be binding must be unequivocal, clearly enunciated and acted upon, and readily ascertainable over a reasonable period of time as a fixed practice accepted by both parties. The past practice under a disputed contract provision is not controlling where the interpretation of the clause has long been the subject of dispute between the parties.[74]

He decided that past practice seemed inconclusive in deciding a case that involved questions of seniority, job classifications, and the filling of vacancies by the posting of jobs for bid. The employer had maintained that jobs in its warehouse were not subject to the bidding procedure; the union had disagreed. Furthermore, the company had permitted bidding on some jobs so that its practice of denying bids had been contaminated by its own actions.

Confusing evidence of past practice was presented to Arbitrator Charles A. Reynard. He acknowledged that where contract language is capable of yielding different interpretations, resort may be made to past practice to resolve the ambiguity. The difficulty here was that the evidence on past practice was in substantial conflict. On two occasions the union had protested the assignment of the challenged work and the work was stopped. The company indicated that the work was stopped, not because of the union's protest, but because it had no further use for equipment involved. The company further presented evidence that it had performed the challenged work with the challenged equipment on several other occasions, that some of these assignments were protested by the union, but in all instances, the company rejected the protests, and the union acquiesced. The union, as complaining party, was held to have failed to sustain its burden of establishing a clear pattern of past practice to support its claim.[75]

An employer may handicap his ability to impose discipline for breach of plant rules by prior conduct in his administration of discipline. This happened to the Coca-Cola Bottling Company in its agreement with the Teamsters Union. Over ten years of contractual relations, the employer had established a custom that no discharge for dishonesty was made without first giving the union the opportunity to investigate and act on its own. Finally, the employer failed to formally notify the union of the company's belief that an employee was guilty of theft until the very day of his discharge. By violating the established custom for handling such cases, the company was held to have breached the labor agreement. Here a past practice, which had been unequivocal, of long duration, and accepted by representatives of both the company and the union had evolved into a binding commitment for the company.[76]

Another past practice was considered as cemented into the relationship between the parties where a successor union incorporated into its first agreement with the company language which had existed for ten years in the agreement with the predecessor union. By failing to raise in negotiations any question about the prior interpretation of the clause, the officers and members of the new local were presumed to have been satisfied with it. Arbitrator Leo C. Brown thus charged the union with knowledge of the prior practice under the same contract language.[77]

In a reporting pay dispute, the union contended that on one occasion under the same contract provision and like circumstances, reporting pay had voluntarily been paid by the employer, thus establishing, by practice, the intent and meaning of the contract. Arbitrator Russell A. Smith could not agree that a single incident established a practice of the parties. As he observed, if the situation were reversed, and payment had been refused on this prior occasion, the union certainly would have been justified in contending here that just because it failed to make a case of the one incident, it should not be precluded from making one in this instance.[78] Obviously, none of the essential ingredients could be found in this dispute.

In order for a past practice to be important in determining the meaning of language, "the practice must be of sufficient generality and duration to imply acceptance of it as an authentic construction of the contract." So holding, Arbitrator Robert E. Mathews ruled in a call-in dispute that an interpretation of the contract contrary to its apparent intent was not justified by the bare showing of the practice of a few payments over an 18-month period.[79]

A union sought payment for 56 hours to an employee who worked six consecutive eight-hour days beginning on Sunday; the governing provision stated that the overtime rate would be paid for Sunday work and work in excess of 40 hours per week, but that the premium would not be granted twice for the same hours. A long-standing practice complicated matters.

The company argued that Sunday premium was paid as daily overtime and therefore should not be counted as a day of work for the purpose of computing overtime over 40 hours. If the overtime was figured on both a weekly and a daily basis, the company would be required to pay a premium on both a daily and a weekly basis.

Looking at the contract language alone, the arbitrator might have been inclined to agree with the union's interpretation, which was that an employee who worked six eight-hour days commencing on a Sunday would be entitled to a payment of 56 hours' pay. However, over 12 years of bargaining, the union had repeatedly sought a change in the contract wording which would have agreed with the interpretation placed upon the disputed clauses by the union. The company had refused to make this language concession. Also throughout their bargaining relationship, the union had lived with the company's interpretation and the past practice which developed as a result. For these reasons, the arbitrator ruled that the company had not violated the overtime premium pay clauses.[80]

This is another example supporting the established concept that practices growing up under one agreement are strengthened when they survive contract negotiations between the parties and continue unchanged into another contract term—particularly where any relevant contract provision is unclear, vague, or ambiguous. Such readoption of identical contract language usually gives rise to the presumption that the parties intended to continue the practices established thereunder.

What this can mean to the parties to the agreement is illustrated where a dispute between A.O. Smith Corporation and the United Electrical, Radio, and Machine Workers Union centered about a contractual phrase that vacation pay should be computed on the basis of "the regularly scheduled work week." The union contended that the phrase meant the regularly scheduled work week of the individual employee, or, at least, of the department. The company claimed that the phrase could mean only the regularly scheduled work week of the entire plant. The method of computation could materially affect the earnings of employees. The section was not as clear as might have been wished, and, on its face, was susceptible to more than one interpretation.

Since the parties had failed to express their intent with clarity in the labor agreement, the ambiguity had to be resolved by reference to the collective bargaining on this subject, and to any relevant past practice. The evidence was clear and undisputed that the language was to be interpreted, as the company contended, to mean the work week scheduled plantwide, rather than by the individual employee or department. The union knew both before and during the negotiation that practice had favored the company's "plantwide" interpretation. Therefore, as the arbitrator Peter M. Kelliher, said:

> In accepting the identical language, without expressing a clear change in intent, the union ran the risk of having any ambiguity in the language resolved on the basis of the contract established by the practice.... Any party desiring a change in application or meaning must assume the responsibility of seeing to it that the wording of the provision involved is qualified or modified to make explicit the change intended.

> It is a well-settled principle of industrial arbitration that where past practice has established a meaning for language that is subsequently used by the parties in a new agreement, the language will be presumed to have the meaning given it by past practice.[81]

The precise question had been placed before another arbitrator in a previous hearing involving the same parties and precisely the same contract language. Only the aggrieved employee was different. There had been an intervening negotiation, and the new agreement repeated the same language. The arbitrator had no choice but to find that on the basis of the prior award and the settled past practice, the construction of the previous agreement had been carried over into the new agreement.[82]

Again, the bridge effect is important, but in this instance it is supported by the additional weight of a prior arbitration award of precedential value.

Arbitrator Whitley P. McCoy stated this principle in the case of Dwight Manufacturing Company and the Textile Workers of America:

> Such practice, on familiar principles of law, constituted a construction of the contract by the parties themselves, and became a part of that contract by virtue of such construction. Therefore, when the identical language, thus construed by the parties, was incorporated into the latest contract, the construction was also reincorporated.[83]

One essential ingredient to make a practice compelling and binding is that it be acquiesced in by the parties. Even where it may have continued for a long period of time with consistent and uniform administration, where either party can demonstrate to an arbitrator long-standing objections to the practice, it often falls. Such was the case at the Hotpoint Company in its agreement with the UAW. Despite a company claim that its practices in vacation administration were long-standing, it could hardly claim the practice had been accepted. The union in its early negotiations with the company, in its presentation of several grievances before an arbitrator, and in the instant case before Arbitrator Otto J. Babb, had definitely objected to this "past practice." Therefore, although it had endured for a considerable period of time, it was rejected.[84]

The intention in reviewing these cases has been to provide a sense of some general standards for the role of past practice in arbitral decisionmaking. Although past practice is not the sole problem for those in the labor-management arena, it certainly must rank high on any list of the more perplexing issues. Generalizations regarding the weight arbiters accord to past practice are not impossible, as many labor relations practitioners are prone to believe. I hope that in some small way I have dismissed from the

minds of some practitioners the notion that arbitrators make
their judgments on cases involving this issue in a capricious
manner.

CITATIONS

1. *Electrical, Radio & Machine Workers* v. *Westinghouse Electric Corporation* – F Supp – (47CCH Lab. Cas. Par 18, 357) (SD NY 1963).

2. Arbitrator S. Wolff in 10 LA 98.

3. Copelof in 13 LA 211; also, Maggs in 17 LA 606, and Klamon in 21 LA 91.

4. Arbitrator Cahn in 29 LA 708; Seward in 12 LA 810.

5. Arbitrator Marshall in 20 LA 212.

6. 23 LA 206; also, Arbitrator Whiting in 5 LA 304 and Holly in 26 LA 325.

7. 23 LA 164; also, Larson in 29 LA 59; Doyle in 22 LA 785; Updegraff in 20 LA 890.

8. 26 LA 146.

9. 26 LA 666.

10. Arbitrator Willcox in 10 LA 371; also, Klamon in 15 LA 782; Warns in 29 LA 324; Pollard in 10 LA 498.

11. Arbitrator Bowles in 23 LA 691.

12. Arbitrator Brecht in 24 LA 199; Morvant in 24 LA 453; Shipman in 10 LA 113; Yeager in 29 LA 487.

13. 7 LA 150; 5 LA 60; and Updegraff in 11 LA 689.

14. 26 LA 638.

15. Arbitrator Platt in 7 LA 764.

16. Arbitrator Killingsworth in 7 LA 334.

17. Arbitrator Healy in 14 LA 787.

18. Arbitrator Howard in 23 LA 440.

19. 28 LA 315.

20. 26 LA 898.

21. Arbitrator Schedler in 37 LA 442; Schmidt in 7 BSA 4975; Donnelly in 25 LA 151; Stutz in 24 LA 883.

22. Arbitrator Wallen in 8 LA 720.

23. Arbitrator Sembower in 29 LA 67.

24. Arbitrator Porter in 22 LA 608; Lennard in 25 LA 118; Aaron in 26 LA 870; Kagel in 24 LA 33.

25. Arbitrator Seward in 30 LA 678; Hogan in 21 LA 713; Lennard in 25 LA 118; Shister in 28 LA 461.

26. Arbitrator Wolff in 27 LA 174; Wallen in 28 LA 491; Holly in 19 LA 815; Hogan in 21 LA 713.

27. Arbitrator Larson in 27 LA 233.

28. Arbitrator Maggs in 19 LA 503; Jones in 24 LA 821; Haughton in
     26 LA 432; Wallen in 28 LA 491; Gray in 26 LA 723; Grant in 19
     LA 219; Wolff in 29 LA 594.

29. Arbitrator Haughton in 26 LA 438; Klamon in 27 LA 57; Kates in
     25 LA 281; Williams in 21 LA 330; Hogan in 21 LA 713.

30. Arbitrator Blair in 23 LA 171; Gray in 26 LA 723; Reid in 22 LA
     124: Coffey in 20 LA 432.

31. Arbitrator Duff in 29 LA 609; McCoy in 27 LA 671.

32. "A Profile of Labor Arbitration," BNA, 166A970 by Edgar L.
     Warren and Irving Bernstein 238 responding Arbitrator..

33. Von Moschzisker Res Adjudicata, 38 Yale Law Journal 299
     (1929); Symposium on Res Adjudicata, 39 Iowa Law Review 213
     (1954).

34. 25 LA 426, Arbitrator Carroll Daugherty.

35. For examples, see 24 LA 193, 32 LA 247, 25 LA 146, 22 LA 181,
     16 LA 74, 22 LA 336. (Many other such cases are found by an
     examination of any volume of published awards.)

36. Erick Heller, Oswald Spengler and the Predicament of the His-
     torical Inauguration in the Disinherited Mind, Farrar, Straus and
     Cudahy (1957).

37. 25 LA 149.

38. 63-1 ARB 8063.

39. 62-2 ARB 8611, 62-2 ARB 8584, 63-2 ARB 8695; see also 11 LA
     945, 25 LA 896, 37 LA 830.

40. 62-3 ARB 8882.

41. 62-3 ARB 8946; see also 39 LA 567, 28 LA 476.

42. 62-3 ARB 8964. For another case between different local unions
     in different plants of the same firm, see 33 LA 25.

43. 24 LA 379, 9 LA 761.

44. For example, 16 LA 111, 16 LA 844, 32 LA 126, 32 LA 156, 26 LA
     84, 26 LA 258, 24 LA 193, 24 LA 181, 23 LA 39.

45. 15 LA 934, Arbitrator Douglas B. Maggs.

46. 16 LA 217, Arbitrator Whitley McCoy.

47. 32 LA 360. For similar rulings, see 16 LA 816, 22 LA 721, 33 LA
     826, 35 LA 826, 37 LA 119.

48. BNA Proceedings of the Eleventh Annual Meeting – National
     Academy of Arbitrators, The Chrysler – UAW Umpire System, by
     David A. Wolff, Louis A. Crane, Howard A. Cole.

49. 9 LA 757, Saul Wallen.

50. Donald Drawford, pages 52– 53, Challenges to Arbitration, Pro-
     ceedings of the Thirteenth Annual Meeting of National Academy
     of Arbitrators, BNA 1960.

51. Sidney Wolff, 14 LA 31 at 34 and 36 (1950).

52.   Milton Schmidt, 7 BSA 4975 (1958), and Donnelly, 25 LA 151 (1955), and Stutz, 24 LA 883 (1955).

53.   Aldrich, 30 LA 851 at 852 (1958) and Slichter, Healy, and Livernash, *The Impact of Collective Bargaining on Management* (Brookings, 1960), p. 311. One arbitrator even found the issue inarbitrable, M. S. Ryder, 22 LA 251. Also R. Feinberg, 13 LA 991 (1949), and P. Kelliher, 24 LA 158, and V. Stouffer, 35 LA 397 (1960).

54.   For Arbitrators who have supported this concept, see Maggs, 19 LA 503, Coffey, 20 LA 432, Kelliher, 24 LA 158.

55.   Hogan, 21 LA 713 (1953).

56.   W. McCoy, 12 LA 707 (1949), and V. Stouffer, 35 LA 397 at 402 (1960).

57.   Coffey, 20 LA 432, Grant, 19 LA 219, Wolff in 27 LA 174, Kelliher in 24 LA 158, Maggs in 19 LA 503, Kornblum in 28 LA 270, Wolff in 29 LA 594, Wallen in 28 LA 491.

58.   Porter in 22 LA 608, Lennard in 25 LA 118, Aaron in 26 LA 870, Kagel in 24 LA 33.

59.   Seward in 30 LA 678, Hogan in 21 LA 713, Lennard in 25 LA 118, Klamon in 27 LA 57, Duff in 29 LA 609, Larson in 27 LA 233, Shister in 28 LA 461.

60.   Wolff in 27 LA 174, Wallen in 28 LA 491, Holly in 19 LA 815, Hogan in 21 LA 713, Blair in 23 LA 171.

61.   Lennard, 25 LA 118 (1955), Larson in 27 LA 233.

62.   Haughton in 26 LA 438, Kalman in 27 LA 57, Kates in 25 LA 281, Williams in 21 LA 330, Hogan in 21 LA 713.

63.   Maggs in 19 LA 503, Jones in 24 LA 821, Haughton in 26 LA 432 and 24 LA 121, Wallen in 28 LA 491, Gray in 26 LA 723, Grant in 19 LA 219, Wolff in 29 LA 594.

64.   Institute of Industrial Relations, Univ. of California, 1960. (Law and National Labor Policy), Vol. 12, p. 143.

65.   28 LA 439.

66.   28 LA 14.

67.   17 LA 81.

68.   28 LA 372.

69.   3 LA 137, see also 3 LA 760.

70.   29 LA 256.

71.   1 LA 313.

72.   23 LA 277.

73.   29 LA 555.

74.   27 LA 762.

75.   27 LA 793.

76.   9 LA 197.

77.   21 LA 524.

78.   22 LA 835.
79.   10 LA 617.
80.   29 LA 45.
81.   23 LA 27.
82.   15 LA 87.
83.   10 LA 786.
84.   23 LA 562.

2

Arbitration and Discipline

Standard of Just Cause

A Bureau of National Affairs survey revealed that 82 percent of 400 representative contracts expressly stipulated some grounds for discharge. A general statement that discharge could be made for "just cause" or "cause" appeared in 71 percent of the agreements. Many also stated one or more specific grounds, but few included a complete listing of actionable offenses or indicated the penalty for particular violations. This is one reason why discharge and discipline continue to be the issues most frequently submitted to arbitration.

Arbitrators are indispensable to a peaceful collective bargaining process. Their responsibility is to determine whether or not the draftsmen of the contract have included a particular issue for arbitral review and, if included, what the remedy should be. The arbitrator is limited to interpreting and applying the collective instrument. His role is not to dispense his own brand of industrial justice; as the Supreme Court has said:

> He may of course look for guidance from many sources, yet his award is legitimate only so long as it draws its essence from the collective bargaining agreement. When the arbitrator's words manifest an infidelity to this obligation, courts have no choice but to refuse enforcement of the award.[1]

The Court also said, in *United Steelworkers of America* v. *Warrior & Gulf Navigation Company,* that section 310 of the LMRA assigns to the courts the duty of determining

41

whether the reluctant party has breached his promise to arbitrate. Arbitration "is a matter of contract and a party cannot be required to submit to arbitration any dispute which he had not agreed to submit."[2] Thus, discipline and discharge cases are excluded from arbitration if the contractual language clearly and explicitly bars them. But the wording must be unmistakable, since the Court has also held that matters should be considered susceptible to arbitration unless expressly excluded.

However, of the 400 labor agreements surveyed, the great majority do provide for arbitration of discipline and discharge disputes. Therefore, the meaning of the term "just cause" or "cause" becomes a factor of substantial import to both parties.

Before exploring how various arbitrators define "just cause," let us glance briefly at agreements that merely state that a discharge must be for "cause." There are arbitrators who have taken the view that, by using the unqualified term "cause," the parties must have envisioned a more flexible standard than would be entailed by the qualified term "just cause."[3] On the other hand, some have equated "cause" with "just cause" or with the standard of "reasonable and sufficient" justification. The single word has also been interpreted as intending a "fair and legitimate" reason—"not merely any reason."[4]

Definitions of Just Cause

What is "just cause"? The answer has been mystifying to management representatives and union officials; elusive to arbitrators. A reading of arbitral opinion produces no standardized definition. Usually the parties to an agreement containing a just cause condition do not give an arbitrator much help on what they consider to be just and fair. This forces him to follow his own judgment, and one individual's concept may differ substantially from another's. Moreover, as one arbitrator has said, in determining just cause where an agreement vests management with the right to discipline, an arbitrator should not substitute his own judgment for management's unless he finds that the employer acted arbitrarily, unreasonably, or in bad faith.[5]

The decisions of arbitrators are binding rulings only on the particular dispute decided; "what constitutes just cause is a matter that must be based on the individual merits of each case."[6] Its outcome will be determined by the particular facts, circumstances, and contractual language, with past practice, the history of negotiations between the parties, and the skill of the advocates influential. For the most part, arbitrators feel free to disregard colleagues' rulings, though they will examine these for guidance. Decisions that deal with comparable contractual situations show the arbitrators the reasoning behind other respected arbitral opinions, and support some general conclusions on what constitutes just and proper cause for discipline and discharge under a labor agreement.

Some Arbitral Views on Just Cause

Under one contract, management had reserved to itself the complete function of discharging employees. The only protection afforded employees was that "A discharge may not be arbitrary or capricious or without just cause." After a frustrating search for a key to the enigma of what just cause is, the arbitrator finally remarked:

> About all that an impartial Arbitrator can do, therefore, is to decide the justice or injustice of the discharge here in question in the light of (a) common sense, (b) common knowledge of generally prevailing industry standards for employee deportment and (c) common understanding ... absent specific criteria mutually agreed on [whereby] an Employer may fairly and justly discharge an employee with seniority rights.[7]

The highly respected arbitrator Harry H. Platt decided a case between the Steelworkers and the Riley Stoker Corporation in which the definition of just cause was at issue. His comments have often been referred to by other practitioners:

It is ordinarily the function of an arbitrator in interpreting a contract provision which requires "sufficient
cause" as a condition precedent to discharge not only
to determine whether the employee involved is guilty
of wrongdoing and, if so, to confirm the employer's
right to discipline where its exercise is essential to the
objective of efficiency, but also [to] safeguard the interests of the discharged employee by making reasonably
sure that the causes for discharge were just and equitable and such as would appeal to reasonable and fair-
minding persons as warranting discharge. To be sure,
no standards exist to aid an arbitrator in finding a
conclusive answer to such a question and, therefore,
perhaps the best he can do is to decide what reasonable men, mindful of the habits and customs of industrial life and of the standards of justice and fair dealing
prevalent in the community, ought to have done under
similar circumstances and in that light to decide
whether the conduct of the discharged employee was
defensible and the disciplinary penalty just.[8]

Another arbitrator has listed the following criteria to guide
him in determining whether a discharge is just or reasonable:

(1) There must be reasonable cause at the time of the
discharge. Thus the employer may not justify a
discharge based on arbitrary or capricious considerations by referring to subsequent developments.

(2) It cannot be said that a disciplinary action has been
based on reasonable cause if management searches
for justifying reasons after taking the action.

(3) Reasonable cause must rest on a valid type of
employee failure, not on his job relationship with
the employer and not on the company's prefer-
ences or predilections.

(4) The search for reasonable cause ordinarily may
not intrude on an employee's personal life.[9]

In deciding a case between the Electric Hose & Rubber
Company and the United Rubber Workers Union, Arbitrator

Irvine L. H. Keerison listed his criteria for evaluating the justness of a discharge or suspension:

> One criterion is that of equal treatment. While this does not mean that all must be judged by the same standards interpreted as giving the same penalties for the same offenses at all times, regardless of extenuating circumstances, it does mean that all must be judged by the same standards as such, and that rules must apply equally to all.

> A second criterion is what often is called the rule of reason. Where even, as is not the case here, a Contract does not contain a specific provision protecting employees against unjust discharge or suspension, the Contract as a whole may be held to afford that protection and to challenge any company procedure that threatens to unjustly deprive employees of rights and privileges contained within the four corners of that document.

> A third criterion is what often is called the test of internal consistency. Whether a company disciplines on a case-by-case basis, or compiles a code of standard violations with appropriate penalties for each, the test is whether or not the pattern of enforcement is consistent.

> A fourth criterion is that guilt is personal. The fact that two or more employees are involved in the same act of misconduct does not necessarily justify the same penalty for all. For one thing, the prior disciplinary record of each involved employee often is considered.[10]

Carroll Daugherty's seven carefully reasoned standards are among the most comprehensive and succinct. For an employer's discipline or discharge to be upheld, all seven questions must be answered in the affirmative. If any one question evokes a negative response, the company's action will either fall or be amended.

(1) Did the employee have foreknowledge that his conduct would be subject to discipline, including possible discharge?

(2) Was the rule he violated reasonably related to the safe, efficient, and orderly operation of the company's business?

(3) Did the company make a reasonable effort before disciplining him to discover whether he in fact did violate this rule?

(4) Was its investigation fair and objective?

(5) Did it obtain substantial evidence that the employee was guilty of the offense with which he was charged?

(6) Was its decision nondiscriminatory?

(7) Was the degree of discipline given him reasonably related to the seriousness of his proven offense and/or to his record with the company?[11]

The Complexity of the Problem

Though certain standards are shared by arbitrators, one may give greater weight to a certain point than do others. Also, some have articulated their criteria more thoroughly than have others. This is one factor that contributes to the enigma of just cause; no universal formulas guide management in establishing and implementing discipline policies. Another factor is that many contracts do not list the rules whose violation will produce discipline, and most do not specify the penalties for infractions.

Some employers pursue the concept of "corrective discipline." Intrinsic in this concept is the requirement that each worker be given fair, objective, and just treatment when a penalty is being imposed. In this connection, management weighs such matters as the individual's length of service and prior work and discipline records in determining what penalty to assess. This alone makes each case independent of others with different facts and circumstances.

When we add to an already complex problem the factor of an outside third party, the arbitrator, with a unique intellectual and psychological makeup, we have pulled together most of the ingredients that produce the enigma of just cause. A partial solution, of course, is for management always to utilize a standard of good and sufficient cause and provide its workers with a full measure of industrial justice.

The Need for a Sound Standard

The union recognizes full well that if the employer has an unlimited right to discharge at will, many important contractual provisions are negated. The seniority provisions of the labor agreement presumably insure an orderly procedure for layoff and recall, but a company allowed to discharge at will without cause can easily ignore this contractual machinery. The company can thus nullify one of the fundamental benefits the worker derives from the contractual relationship: security in his employment status.

The compelling value of the just cause concept to employees can readily be seen when the results of its absence are contemplated. Discharge has sometimes been referred to, perhaps a little overdramatically, as the capital punishment of the labor-management relationship. Certainly the general economic climate has a great bearing on how seriously a worker is affected by a discharge. When the economy is strong and levels of unemployment are low, he can usually obtain another job. Also, good skills will help him find suitable employment that will maintain his basic life style. Moreover, if his job tenure has been relatively brief, the break in service and the resultant loss of accumulated seniority and other benefits may be only a small sacrifice to him. However, the impact of a discharge can be severe if the worker possesses many years of service, does not have substantial skills, and finds himself jobless at a time when the general economy is on a downturn.

In any case, everyone experiences an unpleasant psychological reaction to the stigma of discharge. No matter what the actual circumstances, an employee feels that his neighbors and friends consider him a failure. Often he will feel this way himself and must bear it within his own family. It also adds to his embarrassment in seeking another job.

Although management would hardly consider discharge as equivalent to capital punishment, it must recognize discharge as the severest penalty it can inflict on its workers and that it always creates a hardship, often quite a critical one.

All this explains why the standard of just cause came into being primarily under the influence of unions. For many years before the advent of unionization, management's authoritarian approach to maintaining order and handling personnel intimidated workers. A management that attempted this practice today would soon find itself on a collision course. Today employers generally recognize that workers are human beings first and clock-card numbers second. Supervisors have learned that supporting directives with valid reasons will obtain more positive reactions and that encouraging self-discipline will be much more effective in the long run than will threats and intimidation. In this context, the standard of just cause serves merely as another measure of security, helping insure that management will give employees fair and equal treatment.

The Silent Contract and Just Cause

Arbitrators are divided on the criteria for evaluating discipline and discharge actions under a contract that sets no standards. Although there does appear to be a majority viewpoint, the minority position appears just often enough to confuse the average practitioner.

The majority of decisions hold that even when a contract contains no general limitation on management's right to discharge, a just cause restriction is implied.[12]

One of the most respected arbitration authorities, Meyer S. Ryder, has said:

> In the setting of labor contractual commitments and what they mean to benefit both employer and employee, to not have some reasonable and accepted justifiable basis for the disciplinary severance of an employment relationship is to mortgage the very stability

in the workforce that the productive enterprise must want and have.[13]

Judge Norman N. Eiger, deciding a discharge dispute between Continental Airlines and the Teamsters, commented:

> Discharge is one of the most drastic measures a company can take against an employee. With his discharge comes loss of seniority rights, pay, and all the benefits secured by the employee under the collective bargaining Agreement.
>
> Although the instant Contract has no particular provision that an employee shall not be discharged without just cause, nevertheless, it is the considered opinion of the Arbitrator, in the light of overwhelming legal authority and precedent and in this day of enlightened labor-management relations, that such a provision is implicit and inherent in the Contract in question.
>
> To hold that a company can capriciously at its sole discretion without just cause discharge an employee would in effect nullify the provisions of the Contract entered into by the parties.[14]

Arbitrators agreeing with this viewpoint will examine with extreme care an employer's claim that it has an unchallengeable right under the contract to discharge for any reason, just or unjust. Most arbitrators find it difficult to believe that a union would grant an employer unfettered authority. This does not mean that no labor agreements give the employer the unilateral right to discharge without need for cause, but such agreements are both few and unusual. As Arbitrator Saul Wallen has said, the meaning of the contract viewed as a whole "is that a limitation on the employer's right to discharge was created with the birth of the instrument. Both the necessity for maintaining the integrity of the contract's component parts and the very nature of collective bargaining agreements are the basis for this conclusion."[15]

Where the contract is silent regarding any standard of cause or just cause, one arbitrator found that past practice demonstrated the parties' intentions to have some standard applied.[16]

Majority arbitral opinion holds that if a firm can use discharge to circumvent any right or benefit otherwise extended to employees under a contract, the firm's license is nullified. Most practitioners will also agree that a company does not have this power unless contractual language establishes it beyond any question. But others have held that the absence of any express restriction on management's right to discharge shows an intention for this power to be unlimited. Edgar L. Warren, in a case involving Meletron Corporation, expressed this view:

> While a discharge grievance can be presented, the Company is under no contractual obligation to justify the decision it has made.

> It is also the opinion of the Arbitrator that the security provisions of the Agreement do not modify the Company's right to discharge employees, with or without cause, without having its decision challenged in arbitration.[17]

Discipline and Discharge

The Test of Reasonableness

Management's rules must be reasonable in both context and administration. A rule appropriate in one industrial situation may be quite inappropriate in another. For example, prohibiting smoking is eminently fair and reasonable where the danger of fire and explosion is great, but not where such dangers do not exist. Or the nature of the operations may make absenteeism and moonlighting more critical problems in one industrial situation than in another. Moreover, a just rule can be unjustly implemented—by management's requiring too strict adherence, for example, or imposing overly severe penalties for infractions.

For these reasons, a union customarily reserves the right to challenge company rules and disciplinary actions. In grievance and arbitration procedures, then, the agreement is applied to determine whether a company action was fair and reasonable, whether the right employee was its subject, and whether he was in fact guilty of an infraction.

Safety precautions may be put to the test of reasonableness on the basis of exactly opposing complaints—that they are too lax or that they are too burdensome. Most contracts make the company responsible for making reasonable efforts to provide safe and healthful working conditions. Unfortunately, because a good many employers fail to meet these obligations to the best of their ability, grievances are still numerous. Occasionally, however, a dedicated management will find itself charged with overzealousness. The Bethlehem Steel Corporation issued a rule requiring all employees, except office workers, to wear hard hats and safety glasses at all times. The union contended that the rule constituted a contractual violation. After asserting that the company was in violation by failing to secure its prior agreement on the rule, the union alleged that requiring all employees to use these safety articles at all times was not reasonable or necessary.

The arbitrator's ruling made three points. First, under the contract, the company had the exclusive power to issue safety rules; the union's function was to cooperate with and jointly review the safety program. Second, the rule bore a reasonable relationship to the employer's safety objectives. Third, the company's administration of the rule would be limited by a contractual provision that precluded discipline except for just cause.

Here is an instance of a rule that is reasonable on its face but whose supervisory administration may be adjudged unreasonable. Its application would scarcely be just if an employee were disciplined for removing the hard hat while taking a shower or answering a call of nature or for taking off steamed glasses to clean them. Though upholding the company's right to promulgate such a rule and finding the rule reasonable, the arbitrator did not pass on any individual cases. Each disciplinary action would have to stand on its own merits and meet the test of just cause.

One employer determined it must do something to control excessive absenteeism. The labor agreement expressly gave it the right to make, publish, and enforce reasonable plant rules that did not conflict with the agreement. The union tested the reasonableness of the company's decision that it could discipline and discharge employees for excused as well as unexcused absences. The arbitrator held that when an employee had requested and received management's permission to be off, it could not consider him to have committed an offense, and that penalizing him as though he had was contrary to the contractual requirement of just cause for discipline. The decision, therefore, was that the administration of the rule was unreasonable.

There is a long line of arbitration cases, on the other hand, where the decision has gone the other way. Certainly no business can function efficiently and profitably without a reliable workforce. Excessive absences interfere with work schedules, necessitate replacements and additional manpower, and cause substantial losses of time and money. Therefore, although an employee's absences may be for valid reasons, they may still be considered excessive and unacceptable.

Thus many arbitrators have held that when an individual is absent so often over a continuing period (even excusably and justifiably) that he is of little value and perhaps is actually a hindrance to the company, it may eventually terminate the employment relationship. Such action is most often considered a nondisciplinary discharge.

The reasonableness of a rule that provided for a monetary levy on employees who lost tools through negligence was the issue at another firm. The arbitrator held that the company had not violated the contract by adopting the rule. The agreement, recognizing the employer's right to adopt and enforce reasonable rules for efficient operations, implied that the right could be enforced through disciplinary action. The arbitrator concluded that this contract gave the company under proper circumstances the right to deduct from pay checks for lost tools, and he deemed the rule reasonable in that employees were charged only for negligent loss.

Again where is a rule considered reasonable on its face and necessary because of serious potential operational difficulties and expenses. However, the administration of the rule was another matter. The company did not carry the burden of showing that an employee's loss of the tool was negligent but relied on his not reporting the loss before inventory investigations revealed it. The arbitrator concluded that the employee might simply not have known the tool was missing. The company did not require employees to make frequent inventories of their tools; nor did it give them the opportunity to explain losses. The arbitrator recommended a standardized procedure for soliciting the employees' explanation, to establish that the application of the rule was reasonable.

Ignorance of the Law

In society at large, the citizen who alleges ignorance to defend his violation of a law is seldom excused by law-enforcement people.

A somewhat different condition exists in industrial society: Arbitrators have customarily held that an employee cannot be expected to comply with rules he does not know. Employees are not bound to know particular rules, although serious misconduct may be the subject of disciplinary action, even in the absence of specific regulation. Just cause requires that employees be informed of a rule the infraction of which may result in suspension or discharge, unless conduct is so clearly wrong that specific reference is not necessary.

Rarely have arbitrators upheld a management attempt to discipline an employee for violating a rule that was not adequately promulgated. The employee has a sustainable defense if he can establish that he could not have known of the rule. This is why some employers have chosen to enumerate their factory regulations fully within the labor document itself. Still others publish them in an employee hand-

book, which generally also outlines other conditions and
benefits of the employment relationship. The majority seem
to prefer bulletin boards throughout the operating facility.
In any case, an arbitrator will rarely sustain a disciplinary
action unless management can establish that it has taken
steps to communicate its rules effectively.

Furthermore, most employers have found it advisable
to issue a rule, advise employees of the date it will go into
effect (perhaps one week later), and state that violations
occurring thereafter will result in disciplinary penalties. This
enables employees to make any necessary preparations for
compliance with the rule.

Discharge and Discipline of Union Representatives

The most delicate type of discharge or discipline case is
generally that which finds a union official as target of management's action. The dual role of the union officer, as an
employee and an official of the labor organization, adds a
dimension to his conduct not shared by ordinary employees. As an employee, he has only the rights and privileges of
other employees and is governed by similar rules, but as a
union representative, he enjoys a certain latitude in day-to-
day administration of the contract. The discipline or discharge of such an union official frequently raises the question of whether management's action had antiunion or discriminatory motivation. A related question is whether the
act objected to was performed when he was acting "as an
employee," or "as a union official," which might entitle him
to some special immunity.

Insubordination

In cases where insubordination by union stewards is alleged,
if the steward was acting as an employee, then penalties are
generally considered properly the same as for rank-and-file
employees under similar circumstances. At the Dominion
Electric Company, a union official refused a job assignment

and the arbitrator concluded that the company did not discharge him with intent to discriminate, but rather for his refusal as an individual to carry out a proper order.[18]

Similarly, at American Can Company, the employer was found justified in discharging for "gross and defiant insubordination" a union president who continually left his job without proper leave to investigate grievances.[19]

At Chrysler Corporation, under a contract which obligated the chief steward to report to his foreman the number and nature of grievances he wished to investigate, the employer was found justified in discharging him after his refusal to work overtime on grounds he was investigating grievances, but refused to identify which grievances. It was considered significant that he had been instructed by his foreman to report for the overtime assignment and warned to identify the specific grievances under investigation, return to his job, or be discharged.[20]

In a case with a different twist, the arbitrator sustained the discharge of a union steward who continually functioned in the capacity of a union official outside of a fixed, agreed-upon period established for stewards to discharge their union duties. Although he was acting as a union official, his refusal to stop was in disregard of the contract.[21]

But where the steward is "on union business," and orders given are in conflict with the union's rights, arbitrators will not apply the usual requirement of "obey first, grieve later."

In such a dispute Arbitrator Whitley McCoy articulated this concept:

> There is a clear distinction between the case of a supervisor telling an employee to go back to his job and a supervisor telling the union to stop investigating a grievance. The company and union have met on equal terms and adopted a contract recognizing each other's rights. Each has its dignity to uphold. Organizations and corporations can act only through agents and representatives. When the duly authorized representative of the company told the duly authorized representative of the

union to stop investigating a grievance, it was the company issuing orders to the union. . . . If he [steward]
could rightly be penalized, it would put the entire
grievance machinery, set up by agreement of the parties
at the highest levels, at the mercy of supervisors, with
the possibility of great harm to the relations of the
parties, even to a complete breakdown of the grievance
machinery.[22]

In another case where a steward was disciplined for leaving
his work station without permission, the arbitrator over-
turned the suspension due to a plant practice which permitted stewards to leave their work point for purposes of
grievance handling and go to the foreman without first
obtaining permission. This arbitrator considered it:

unrealistic to strictly interpret the contract to the effect that the committeeman, learning of a grievance
arising within his department and jurisdiction as a
union representative, must remain at his machine until
the foreman comes to his machine and the committeeman is able to request permission to leave his machine
to work on the grievance.[23]

Arbitrator Dudley Whiting rendered a different type of remedy where a union committeeman was discharged for
refusing to perform assigned work which he believed was
not covered by his classification. Arbitrator Whiting, con-
cluding that the committeeman's trouble was due to overzealousness in his union office, reinstated him without back
pay—with the condition that he resign as union committeeman and pledge to remain out of such office.[24]

Ignorance of Law Is Excuse

Arbitrators will frequently weigh the union official's length
of time in office and consider his degree of sophistication
and familiarity with the scope of his union authority. A new
steward's improprieties in office may be excused, or partially justified, because he is not completely informed. Such
was the story at International Harvester when a union

committeeman was disciplined for violating a company rule forbidding distribution of handbills on company property. The committeeman had acted in the honest belief he was within his rights because of a recent NLRB decision involving a different company, which found illegal the company order prohibiting distribution of union leaflets on company parking lots.[25]

Arbitrator Clarence Updegraff went another large step further in resolving a dispute over a discharged steward who, on his first day in office, told his foreman he was entitled to go where he pleased and proceeded to "roam" up and down, in disregard of his foreman's repeated orders. Although he censured the behavior of this steward, Updegraff said:

> He would nevertheless have taken immediate proper directions from his own chief within the union, the divisional steward. However, this opportunity to give the inexperienced steward timely correction was ignored by the foreman. The green steward was given a further opportunity to repeat his mistake and to sink further into the consequences of his blunder.... Modern personnel relations require from both sides and their representatives at least a reasonable degree of sympathetic tolerance. On the night of the dispute, S_____was an inexperienced, newly appointed steward. *Management appears to have been guilty almost of entrapment of the steward into a harsh consequence of an ignorant mistake, instead of cooperating in a charitable and tolerant effort to correct his erroneous assumptions.*[26] (Emphasis supplied).

Although most arbiters would not go quite so far, the majority generally give ample consideration to the factor of inexperience in union officials. Arbitrator R. Hayes, for instance, reinstated discharged union officers even though evidence established they had instigated and participated in a strike in violation of the contract. The mitigating circumstances were that (1) the union officers were inexperienced, (2) the employer's operations, local union, and contract

were new, and (3) accumulated grievances had caused employee unrest.[27]

Countermanding Management's Orders

Arbitrators appear to be unanimous on the impropriety of
the union countermanding management's orders, so long as
the order deals with matters generally falling within management's domain. Harry Shulman, a truly great statesman in
the arbitration process and former umpire with the Ford
Motor Company and UAW, articulated this wisdom:

> No committeeman or other union officer is entitled to
> instruct employees to disobey supervision's orders no
> matter how strongly he may believe that the orders are
> in violation of agreement. If he believes that an impro-
> per order has been issued, his course is to take the
> matter up with supervision and to seek to effect an
> adjustment. Failing to effect an adjustment, he may file
> a grievance. But he may not tell the employee to disre-
> gard the order.[28]

In a similar dispute, although Arbitrator Feinberg reduced a
discharge to suspension, he strongly censured a union shop
chairman:

> Certainly, a shop chairman has no right to counter-
> mand instructions given by management's representa-
> tives, whether or not he believes those instructions
> contrary to the terms of the collective bargaining
> agreement. . . . Any other arrangement would result in a
> chaotic condition in the plant and seriously interfere
> with production.[29]

Union Official's Responsibility Greater

Arbitrators generally recognize that local union officials not
only must perform their regular jobs, but also carry an
additional burden of enforcing the contract and influencing
other employees to comply with its terms. Where a union
official participates in an unauthorized work stoppage, his
offense is graver than that of other employees.[30]

This concept was voiced by Arbitrator Arthur Miller.

The employer had suspended a shop steward for engaging in a strike, in violation of the agreement. In his award, Miller said:

> The proposition that affirmative obligations of leadership in upholding the grievance procedure and opposing work stoppages devolved upon an employee, who by reason of seniority and status as a union officer must be held to have achieved a position of influence, has hitherto found acceptance under this and other agreements. Implicit in it is the thought that if those prominent and influential in the affairs of the union fail to so support these vital provisions of the agreement, the parties' expectations that they will be complied with during the life of the agreement become altogether illusory.[31]

Some arbitrators have even viewed a union official's passive behavior in the face of known employee contract violations as a type of "negative leadership." Where the local union president, union committeeman, and shop steward were disciplined for failing attempts to prevent unauthorized work stoppage, Arbitrator Pearce Davis said:

> Local union officials are the spokesmen for the workers. They are their leaders. They, therefore, have responsibilities over and beyond those of the rank and file. Local union officials are obligated aggressively to oppose actions that violate commitments undertaken in good faith. Local union officials are bound by virtue of their office to set personal examples of opposition to contract violation. They cannot be passive; they must vigorously seek to prevent contract violations by their constituents.[32]

Union officials also have been held answerable for their personal behavior in carrying out union duties. Despite the relaxed usage of shop vernacular, arbitrators have upheld discharge of stewards for insulting, abusive, and intimidating verbal attacks on members of management.[33] On the other hand, an employer was not sustained in his attempt to discharge a union official who instigated filing of a large number of grievances.[34]

Though cases involving discharge and discipline for union activities still arise frequently, arbitrators generally concur in their views on the bounds of union authority and the degree of behavioral freedom of the union representative. They impose the same criterion of "just cause" where a steward is disciplined for alleged misconduct "as an employee."

When a union claims antiunion discrimination in the absence of conclusive evidence, the burden of proof falls on the union.

CITATIONS

1. 46 LRRM 2416.
2. *Ibid.*
3. 29 LA 458 and 22 LA 756.
4. 24 LA 1 and 453 and 29 LA 567.
5. 45 LA 1124; see also 39 LA 931.
6. 2 LA 558.
7. 10 LA 207.
8. 7 LA 764.
9. 29 LA 451.
10. 47 LA 1104.
11. 45 LA 515 and 42 LA 555.
12. 24 LA 630 and 22 LA 756 (for examples).
13. 36 LA 552.
14. 38 LA 778.
15. 13 LA 747.
16. Chapter 6, F, for further discussion.
17. 24 LA 680.
18. J. Gross in 20 LA 749.
19. D. Kornblum in 34 LA 262.
20. D. Wolff in 33 LA 112.
21. J. Justin in 10 LA 265. (For other cases where discipline was imposed upon union representatives while "acting as an employee," see 28 LA 543, 15 LA 842, 1 LA 447, 9 LA 765, and 43 LA 46.) For a contrary opinion, see 17 LA 199.
22. W. McCoy in 16 LA 307, also see 39 LA 238.
23. P. Williams in 42 LA 70.

24.   D. Whiting in 10 LA 965.

25.   H. Platt in 21 LA 10. (For similar cases, see 32 LA 144, 14 LA 925.)

26.   Updegraff in 10 LA 355, also see 9 LA 861.

27.   R. Hayes in 33 LA 103.

28.   H. Shulman in 3 LA 779.

29.   Feinberg in 9 LA 861. (For a decision that this principle does not apply to "action falling primarily within the union's domain," see Shulman in 10 LA 213.)

30.   4 LA 744, 21 LA 421, 16 LA 99, 21 LA 843, 21 LA 239, 9 LA 447, 42 LA 131, 42 LA 142, 42 LA 328, 42 LA 923, 13 LA 304, 30 LA 181, 30 LA 250.

31.   28 LA 369; also, 35 LA 699, 20 LA 875.

32.   28 LA 782, 16 LA 99, 29 LA 622, 43 LA 608, 8 LA 758.

33.   9 LA 563; also, 25 LRRM 1381.

34.   37 LA 1076.

3
Arbitrability

The question of the arbitrability of given issues is considered in about one of every ten arbitration clauses in manufacturing agreements and one of every eight in non-manufacturing contracts. These represent substantial increases over the corresponding percentages of only a few years ago. Most such provisions state that the question of arbitrability is one for the arbitrator himself to decide; a very few require a court proceeding.[1]

A contract with the Ladies' Garment Workers, for example, includes a clause that the Impartial Chairman shall have exclusive jurisdiction to determine the arbitrability (substantive or procedural) of any complaint, dispute, or grievance thereunder, and his decision shall be final and binding.[2] This provision would appear to foreclose either party from at any time referring the question of arbitrability to the courts.

In the following example of one of the few collective bargaining agreements providing that such questions be referred to court, the parties may agree to do otherwise: "Any dispute as to the arbitrability of a given matter shall be resolved by a court of competent jurisdiction and not by an arbitrator, unless the parties specifically agree otherwise in writing."[3]

In still another arrangement, either party may seek a judicial determination, but only after an arbitrator has submitted his decision:

> If the Company believes the stated dispute is not arbitrable, it shall advise the Union within five working

days after receipt of the request for arbitration stating its reasons therefore. If the Union decides to proceed with the arbitration, it will advise the Company in writing within five working days after receipt of the Company's notice that the Company believes the dispute is not arbitrable. The arbitration will proceed in the following manner:

(a) The arbitrator will be required to rule first on arbitrability. If he finds in the affirmative, he shall then rule on the merits of the grievance at issue.

(b) If either party challenges the arbitrator's finding regarding the arbitrability, it may within thirty calendar days after receipt of the award, file suit in a court of competent jurisdiction to seek a judicial determination of the arbitrability of the subject matter. The Court in its determination shall be entitled to treat the matter as though originally submitted to it and neither the record of the arbitration nor the finding of the arbitrator shall be given any consideration by the Court.[4]

The clause appears to give to the party contesting arbitrability "two bites at the apple." Few agreements make such elaborate arrangements beforehand; only about one in ten mention a method for obtaining final disposition of any question of arbitrability. This does not mean that parties without contract coverage are left without avenues of relief; it merely means that they either have not contemplated the problem or have not formalized an approach.

Complaints about the contract should not be steered toward the courts unless there is a question of substantive or procedural problems outside the arbitrator's jurisdiction and authority. The court will usually refer the matter back to the arbitration process, particularly if the grievance and arbitration provisions of the contract cover the dispute.

The law of the Steelworkers Trilogy is predicated in part upon the proposition that labor arbitrators are better equipped than judges to deal with questions of contract interpretation. Chief Judge Douglas's opinion in *Warrior and Gulf* tells us that arbitrators perform functions that are "not normal to the courts," that the considerations that help arbitrators fashion judgments may be "foreign to the competence of the courts," and that arbitrators have a knowledge of "industrial common law" and the effects of a particular measure on productivity, shop morale, and intra-plant tensions which even the ablest judge cannot bring to bear.[5]

The Supreme Court has also stated that grievances are not to be compelled to arbitration when they are "so plainly unreasonable that the subject matter of the dispute must be regarded as nonarbitrable because it can be seen in advance that no award to the union would receive judicial sanction."[6]

A collective bargaining agreement typically has a dual purpose: (1) It fixes the substantive terms of employment to prevail in the enterprise, and (2) it establishes the procedural means for resolving disputes arising from the interpretation or application of those terms.

Despite the Steelworkers Trilogy opinions, in *Enterprise Wheel and Car,* the court offered a word of caution:

> An arbitrator is confined to interpretation and application of the collective bargaining agreement; he does not sit to dispense his own brand of industrial justice. He may of course look for guidance from many sources yet his award is legitimate only so long as it draws its essence from the collective bargaining agreement. When the arbitrator's words manifest an infidelity to this obligation, courts have no choice but to refuse enforcement of the award.[7]

Unless the parties expressly exclude a matter from arbitration, the court will conclude that they intended to make it subject to arbitration. Therefore, the federal courts appear to limit themselves to determining whether a contract which contains an arbitration clause is in force, whether there has been a violation, and whether the violation is within the scope of the contract. In considering whether to

compel arbitration, the courts have been instructed by the
United States Supreme Court not to inquire into the merits
of the grievance, but simply to determine whether the claim
itself is covered by the contract.

In addition to these general principles, the courts have
established certain specific criteria for determining whether
to order arbitration. Taken together, these cases comprise a
new body of law covering arbitrability. Briefly, they establish:

(1) If a contract has an arbitration clause and if the
contract covers the subject matter in dispute, the
court should order arbitration without considering the merits of the claim.

(2) An award limited to the "interpretation and application of the collective bargaining agreement" will
be enforced without any review by the court of
the reasoning leading to that award.

(3) Issues of damages for violation of a no-strike
clause will be treated by the courts just as any
other issue. That is, the court will decide whether
the contract refers such issues to the arbitration
process. If so, the issue will be arbitrated. If not,
the court will decide it.

(4) The arbitrator, not the courts, decides issues of
compliance with the contract's procedural requirements.

(5) State courts have concurrent jurisdiction with the
federal courts in suits for breaches of agreement.
But the state courts must apply federal law in any
situation where state and federal laws conflict.

(6) An award which is beyond the scope of the collec-
tive-bargaining agreement may be set aside by the
courts. However, the courts may not review the
reasoning pursued by the arbitrator in making the
award. [8]

Resistance to arbitration may be based first on the claim that
particular subject matters have been excluded from the
promise to arbitrate; for example, merit increases, discharge

for cause, contracting out of work, methods of performing an operation. This is the question of substantive arbitrability: Is the subject within or without the promise to arbitrate?

Second, resistance to arbitration may be based on the claim that the steps preliminary to arbitration have not been followed—that the grievance or arbitration request was not submitted or advanced within prescribed time limits, for instance. This is the procedural question: Was there compliance with the conditions precedent to arbitration?[9]

Meeting Precedent Conditions

There are any number of contractual provisions that could impose conditions on one or the other party as the case develops and proceeds toward eventual arbitration. For example, a contract states that a grievance must be filed within ten days of the occurrence of the event on which it is based, and one is filed six months later—long after the union had knowledge of it. Is it arbitrable?

Another contract states that the employee must be signatory to his grievance, but a grievance is signed by a union committeeman on the employee's behalf. Is it arbitrable?

In a four-step grievance procedure, the union demands arbitration immediately after filing its complaint, skipping all the intervening contractual steps. Will it ultimately prove to be nonarbitrable?

In the absence of a specified time limit for invoking arbitration, is a reasonable time to be inferred? What constitutes a reasonable time?

It is plain that questions of procedure deal with the minutiae of the arbitration process. They are the details of a scheme that, in its overall aspect, is taken for granted as the method of dispute settlement. For example, the question of whether a reasonable time limit to invoke arbitration is to be assumed in the absence of a specifically prescribed time is answered, in major part, by a judgment about the function of grievance handling. A valid judgment may be that a grievance should be handled promptly or be

considered dropped; avoidable delay should be discouraged, for dilatory handling allows an unhealthy accumulation of stale grievances. Therefore, arbitration should be
invoked within a reasonable time or not at all. This is a
value subsumed under the arbitral scheme. Yet questions
of fact are highly particularized. What constitutes a reasonable time, for example, is almost entirely related to the
special circumstances of the individual situation.[10]

The ways in which some of these procedural questions
have been answered by arbitrators are worth reviewing. A
procedural defect not challenged in time may be excused.
At McLouth Steel Corporation, an arbitrator refused to dis-
miss a grievance when the protest against improper filing
was not made until the arbitration hearing. It was held that
such procedural issues are considered to have been waived
if not raised in the previous grievance steps.[11] A preponderance of arbitrators in a large number of published decisions
have concurred with this concept.[12]

With clear contract language delineating the proper
grievance process, most arbitrators will rule that the parties
themselves have established the procedural requirements,
and, failure to protest an infraction in time results in waiver.
As Arbitrator Langston T. Hawley ruled:

> The Company is also contending that the grievance
> should be dismissed because it is not signed, in accor-
> dance with Article XXIX, Section 1 of the Agreement, by
> the aggrieved employee. The arbitrator believes that the
> grievance should be handled on its merits and not
> dismissed on technical grounds. This grievance was
> processed through all steps of the contract prior to its
> submission to arbitration. The Company had five
> months prior to the hearing to raise objection on the
> grounds now being urged and yet its first objection was
> made known to the Union at the time of the hearing. In
> the light of these facts, the arbitrator believes that the
> signature on the grievance of an authorized representa-
> tive of the aggrieved employee is sufficient.[13]

In addition to waivers of this type, there are a variety of other procedural problems, a few of which merit examination. The rulings are often in contrast. Arbitrator Clare B. McDermott in a case between the U.S. Steel Corporation and the United Steelworkers stated:

> The grievance in Case USS-5145-H was filed by thirteen Grievance Committeemen, attempting to allege a violation of an obligation of "the company to the Union as such," under Section 60E, on behalf of all other unnamed employees who did not receive Labor Day holiday pay and who neither filed individual grievances nor signed one of the seven grievances in USS-5145-H.
>
> From the beginning, Management has insisted that this is an improper subject matter for a union grievance under Section 6-E. When the defect was pointed out in Step 3, the Union said it could name individual employees referred to and their particular circumstances, and the employees so identified. No such identification was given. Holiday pay provisions of the Agreement can be applied only in light of specific fact situations, which are of nearly infinite variety, some of which would qualify an employee for holiday pay and others of which would not. Thus, the grievance in USS-5145-H, without stating the particular situations of any named aggrieved employees, really does not present any holiday pay question which this Board can decide, and does not "allege a violation of the obligations of the company to the union as such." Accordingly, it will be dismissed.[14]

In contrast, though the facts were somewhat different, Arbitrator Saul Wallen found a grievance did meet the procedural requirements for detail. He stated:

> Article XXI, Section 7 (c) requires that a written grievance "be in such detail as to identify the nature of the complaint, the name of the aggrieved employee or employees, the date and the place of the complaint." The company objects to the grievance on the grounds that it did not specifically list the names of the grievants

but instead had a seniority roster of Operators ap-
pended to it. We find that the grievance filed is sufficiently definite for the company to identify the persons
who actually were discharged and constituted sufficient notice of the union's challenge of that action. The
inclusion of the names of those not discharged does
not detract from the validity of the protest for those
who were. Thus, the grievance meets the requirements
of Section 7 (c).[15]

A careful examination of the two awards readily reveals the
rationale employed by two competent arbitrators. Although
the factual differences were not substantial, they were
clearly sufficient to produce different findings.

In the next two cases, the question was whether a
regulating agreement existed at all.

A grievance arose after a contract had expired and
before the parties had agreed to abide by the old contract
pending a new one. It was ruled arbitrable. The influencing
factor was that a supervisor answered the grievance in
accordance with contractual procedures after the parties
had agreed to be bound by the old contract; the arbitrator
considered the company bound to arbitrate and obligated
to follow each procedural step after the supervisor's
"answer."[16]

In another situation, a discharge grievance was held
arbitrable even though the discharge occurred before the
employer and the union had executed their contract: (1)
The parties had operated in accordance with the contracts
in effect between other contractors and unions at the job
site before signing their own identical agreement; (2) the
union had attempted to settle the discharge dispute through
contractual grievance procedures, and the employer had
responded on that basis, thereby implicitly acknowledging
that contract procedures applied; and finally (3) the employer did not raise the question of arbitrability until the
arbitration hearing.[17] Even if this last factor had not been in
the picture, the outcome would probably not have been
much different.

Given the types of questions involved in procedural arbitrability, are they more properly resolved by judges or by arbitrators?

In *Livingston* v. *John Wiley and Sons,* the Second Court of Appeals said:

> Indeed, it may well be that the arbitrator can make his most important contribution to industrial peace by a fair, impartial, and well-informed decision of these very procedural matters. To hold matters of procedure to be beyond the competence of the arbitrator to decide would, we think, rob the parties of the advantages they have bargained for, that is to say, the determination of the issues between them by an arbitrator and not by a court. A contrary decision would emasculate the arbitration provisions of the contract. It is of the essence of arbitration that it be speedy and that the source of friction between the parties be promptly eliminated. . . . The numerous cases involving the great variety of procedural niceties . . . make it abundantly clear that, were we to decide that procedural questions under an arbitration clause of a collective bargaining agreement are for the court, we would open the door wide to all sorts of technical obstructionism.[18]

In other words, the promise to arbitrate the merits of disputes evidences a fundamental commitment to the arbitral process; procedural questions, being secondary, have been entrusted to the arbitrator as part of the whole scheme.

Issue Inside or Outside Scope of Arbitration

Perhaps the most frequent claim for nonarbitrability is that the issue is not covered by the contract. In *Warrior and Gulf,* the company argued that subcontracting was purely a management function not limited by the labor agreement. The union argued that the company violated the contract by contracting-out. The arbitration provision at Warrior and Gulf read as follows:

Issues which conflict with any federal statute in its application as established by Court procedure or matters which are strictly a function of management shall not be subject to arbitration under this section.

Should differences arise between the Company and the Union or its members employed by the Company as to the meaning and application of the provisions of this Agreement, or should any local trouble of any kind arise, there shall be no suspension of work on account of such differences but an earnest effort shall be made to settle such differences immediately in the following manner:

> If agreement has not been reached the matter shall be referred to an impartial umpire for decision. The parties shall meet to decide on an umpire acceptable to both. If no agreement on selection of an umpire is reached, the parties shall jointly petition the United States Conciliation Service for suggestion of a list of umpires from which selection shall be made. The decision of the umpire shall be final.

The limitation is primarily expressed in the phrase "or matters which are strictly a function of management shall not be subject to arbitration under this section."

The Supreme Court said that the limitation excluded only some issues from arbitration. Regrettably, the exact boundaries of the exclusion are unclear. The Court stated: "Apart from matters that the parties specifically exclude, all of the questions on which the parties disagree must therefore come within the scope of the grievance and arbitration provisions of the collective agreement." What does this mean? Basically, the conclusion was that an arbitrator may determine what constitutes a management function, because it involves a determination of the "meaning and application" of the contract.

The Court's ruling in no way vitiated the force of the management-rights clause; it merely assigned the issue to the arbitration process as the proper forum.

The scope of management rights and operating clauses may also influence whether the issue raises a substantive question. Essentially, the claim in Warrior and Gulf was that subcontracting was a matter outside the contract and, therefore, not within the arbitrator's jurisdiction. The function of the court is limited: it may determine only whether a party seeking arbitration is making a claim that on its face is governed by the contract. The arbitrators decide the merits.

Decisions on substantive arbitrability may either uphold the claim or reject it as nonarbitrable on its merits. A sampling of both types is useful in order to discern the rationale behind them.

An employer demanded that the union be required to furnish to employees who were not union members the funeral benefits and free periodicals furnished to members. The company's theory was that the contract in general as well as the contract's union-security provisions obligated the union to do so in consideration of the fact that such employees had to pay the union a sum equal to period dues paid by members. The contract did not expressly or by "any interpretation to which the language is susceptible" permit the arbitrator to confer on nonmembers the benefits that under the union's constitution were available to members only.[19]

Another employer's refusal to allow an employee to return to work after a two-year absence caused by a nonoccupational illness was held not arbitrable. Under the agreement, an employee who was not able to work due to nonoccupational illness was to remain on the payroll for 90 days and "his status thereafter shall become a subject of negotiations between the company and the union." The contract merely required the employer to negotiate with the union concerning the return to work of the employee. Once that was done, as it had been here, the employer had no further obligation. The arbiter held that the contract did not require that such negotiations result in agreement or provide that failure to reach agreement was a matter for arbitration.[20]

Occasionally, the conduct or alleged misconduct of a management representative will provoke a grievance. Of course, management should take the necessary steps to censure and correct any instance of supervisory misconduct. However, in the overwhelming majority of such cases the arbitrability of which was contested by management, the arbitrator has most often ruled against the union—unless the parties had agreed by contract or otherwise to give him jurisdiction.

Typical of common sense arbitral rulings in this area was a King Powder Company case where a grievance demanded the discharge of a foreman for using abusive language and improperly docking wages. Arbitrator Dudley Whiting, an experienced and capable member of the National Academy of Arbitrators, commented:

> It is a fundamental principle of American industry that the selection and retention of foremen or other supervisory personnel is the sole prerogative of management, particularly where they are excluded from the benefits of the collective bargaining agreement covering other employees. There is no doubt that the union may not, as a matter of right, demand the dismissal or demotion of a foreman and that such a demand is not a proper subject matter for a grievance.[21]

Yet whether the employer had the right to retire an employee for reasons of age was considered arbitrable under a contract defining "grievance" as "any dispute involving the effect, interpretation, application, claim of breach or violation of the contract and allowing arbitration of any and all grievances so defined." The mere fact that the agreement contained no provision specifically dealing with retirement did not itself preclude the matter from arbitration.[22]

A dispute over the employer's failure to grant maternity leaves was deemed arbitrable, notwithstanding the fact that pregnancy was not listed in the contract as one of the justifications for a leave of absence. The deciding factor was that the subject of leaves as such was dealt with in the contract and was, therefore, in the view of the arbitrator, a matter over which management did not have unlimited discretion.[23]

In a final example, the issue was whether an employee injured in the course of his employment was entitled to the difference between his regular wages and workmen's compensation benefits. Despite the employer's claim that the agreement did not require such pay, the issue was held arbitrable because the contract allowed for arbitration of all differences, disputes, or grievances pertaining to the terms of the contract. However, the arbitrator made it clear that in passing on the question of arbitrability, he was not prejudging the issue itself.[24]

Merits Versus Threshold Issue

When the validity of a grievance is questioned for procedural or substantive reasons, there are two potential issues presented to the arbitrator. First, is the grievance procedurally or substantively faulty to a degree that renders it nonarbitrable? If it is deemed arbitrable, has the claim sufficient merit to be sustained? Several results are possible. If the employer is raising the procedural issue, seeking to have the grievance denied on the procedural question as well as on its merits, the company has two opportunities to have an award in its favor: the union has to survive two tests to achieve its objective.

Of course, the employer may lose on both counts. However, the point should be made that a grievance may raise technical questions about arbitrability and at the same time have intrinsic merits, with both facts recognized by the employer. For example, an employee may be discharged improperly and without sufficient cause—or without any cause at all for that matter; because of contractually improper processing and grievance handling, he may never have his case heard or decided on its merits by reason of it being deemed nonarbitrable. This is an example of one of the inequities of the system for which few acceptable solutions have been found.

In order to have sufficient authority, the arbitrator must be appointed in accordance with the terms of the contract. If his appointment does not square with those requirements, his authority may be invalid and his award unenforceable.

If an appointing agency is empowered to make an arbitral selection for the parties, and that agency does not comply with the contract, the appointment most likely would be invalid. Also, if by the contractual arrangement it is merely to supply names, the agency could not make an appointment if one party refused to participate in the selection process. If the agency makes an appointment, a party must then decide whether it will participate in a hearing or allow it to proceed without him. However, in view of the Steelworkers Trilogy and subsequent cases, it would appear that, if the appointment is procedurally invalid and therefore no award could be enforceable, the courts would probably set aside any award. However, in view of the Steelworkers Trilogy and subsequent cases, it would appear that, if the appointment is procedurally correct and the arbitrator is satisfied after an ex parte hearing that the issue is arbitrable, the courts will probably refuse to review a claim that the subject matter was excluded from arbitration by the contract.

In one major labor agreement, the arbitrability of the dispute is to be decided before it is considered on its merits:

> If either party shall claim before the Arbitrator that a particular grievance fails to meet the tests of arbitrability . . . the Arbitrator shall proceed to decide such issue before proceeding to hear the case upon the merits. . . . In any case where the Arbitrator determines that such grievance fails to meet said tests of arbitrability he shall refer the case back to the parties without a decision or recommendation on its merits.[25]

This language clearly restrains the arbitrator from rendering a decision on the merits of a case that he has found nonarbitrable. However, it may leave certain other questions unanswered.

One might infer from the contract that both issues—arbitrability and merits, as well as the arguments for and against them—are to be presented to the arbitrator at the same hearing. Or can the threshold issue of arbitrability be presented in a separate hearing before any hearing on the merits? Such an approach is often in the best interests of the party contesting arbitrability. The arbitrator may prefer to consider both issues at one time, thus saving himself time and travel; the arbitrator, however, is a servant to the parties—if their mandate is that the issues be heard separately, he must abide by that arrangement.

Dividing the case into two distinct hearings is sometimes viewed as desirable for psychological reasons. Arbitrators are only human after all. The arbitrator would not be influenced by the merits of the case while considering the purely technical arguments about arbitrability. After having heard both cases in full, the arbitrator would have to be extraordinarily well-disciplined to keep the two issues segregated. And the closer the decision on arbitrability, surely the more difficult it is for the arbitrator to rule a case nonarbitrable when it appears to have substantive merits.

These are valid considerations when the parties weigh a decision to combine or separate the issues.

The parties may mutually agree on two hearings. If so, the arbitrator is originally presented only with positions, arguments, and evidence, on the procedural arbitrability question. Only so much of the merits is discussed as is necessary to deal with the threshold question. Only if the finding is in favor of arbitrability is another hearing necessary. The parties may then choose to present the dispute on its merits to a different arbitrator.

There is one other adversary approach to this question of threshold issue versus merits. It involves some willingness to engage in brinksmanship.

If management is adamant in its desire for two separate hearings, it should advise the union of its stand during grievance processing and prearbitration discussions. This should be made clear to the agency selecting the arbitrator or submitting panels of names. It should be made clear to the arbitrator selected, before and during the hearing on the threshold question. He should be advised that he is not empowered to consider the merits of the dispute. He should be advised at the outset of the hearing of any party's intention to withdraw at the close of the hearing on the initial issue and of the party's refusal to be bound by any subsequent ex parte decision. At the appropriate time, the party should leave—and perhaps pray a little.

The arbitrator will usually try to persuade the parties to do it all in one sitting. That is understandable. Also, he will usually not proceed with a hearing from which one party is absent, especially if there is any doubt about his having been given jurisdiction over the second issue. However, if he has been given jurisdiction over that issue, the party is foolhardy to attempt the ex parte approach, and its chances for a favorable outcome are extremely doubtful.

Should the arbiter rule on arbitrability before either party presents its case with regard to merits, or should he reserve his conclusions on the threshold question until the full case, including merits, has been completely presented? Professionals operate from different schools of thought.

Arbitrator Harry Dworkin believes that the ruling on arbitrability should be made before the presentation of the case on the merits:

> The Chairman is of the opinion that when a party raises the issue of arbitrability, it is better practice to pass upon this issue at the time it is presented, and before hearing the dispute on the merits, for the reason that whenever possible, parties should have the right to an interim decision or ruling until after the conclusion of the hearing.[26]

Arbitrator Douglas B. Maggs speaks for the point of view that the ruling on arbitrability may be reserved until the full case has been heard. In a dispute involving Barbet Mills, Inc., he remarked:

> The arbitrator may properly reserve his ruling upon arbitrability until after he has heard evidence and ar-

gument upon its merits. A contrary rule would cause needless delay and expense, necessitating two hearings whenever the arbitrator needed time to consider the question of arbitrability. Furthermore, in many cases, it is only after a hearing on the merits has informed the arbitrator of the nature of the dispute that he is in a position to determine whether it is of the kind covered by the agreement to arbitrate.... This procedure does not, of course, preclude the party who loses from obtaining any judicial review of the arbitrator's decision to which it is entitled by law; to reassure the company about this I explicitly rule that its participation in the hearing upon the merits would not constitute a waiver of its objections to arbitrability.[27]

Dworkin and Maggs have clearly different points of view. As advocate and as arbitrator, I have held both points of view, depending upon my role at the time. As advocate, I favored Dworkin's view, almost always urging the arbitrator to order a total separation of the issues. However, as arbitrator, I was most often inclined to allow that one's position on this particular question is somewhat influenced by the chair he is occupying at the arbitral hearing table.

There is a commonsense middle ground between these two positions: the choice should be based on consideration of all the circumstances of the particular dispute. This procedure is followed by the Connecticut State Board of Mediation, which states:

The Board will inform the party protesting arbitrability that it will be permitted to raise that issue at the hearing. The Board will then first hear arguments on arbitrability before it proceeds to the merits of the dispute. The Board makes clear that at the hearing both parties must be prepared to proceed on the merits after the Board has heard them on arbitrability.

After the case on arbitrability has been presented, the Board will assess the circumstances then obtaining to determine if it will proceed directly to the merits.

Under its policy, the Board reserves the right either to require the parties to go forward on the merits at the same hearing or to determine that the decision on arbitrability should be made first before proceeding on the merits.[28]

This is certainly a more flexible arrangement. Nevertheless, it fails to meet the special needs of the party definitely committed to the separation of issues or one determined to see them treated together.

In any case, the overwhelming majority of published conclusions shows that arbitrators customarily separate the two issues in their written opinions, answering the question of arbitrability before ruling on the merits of the case.

CITATIONS

1.   Bureau of National Affairs, CBNC, No. 397, BNA, 1969.

2.   Labor Agreement between National Dress Manufacturers Association and International Ladies Garment Workers Union, 1966.

3.   Labor Agreement between Gulf Oil Corp. Port Arthur Refinery and OCAW, 1970.

4.   Labor Agreement between Coleman Company, Inc., and Tool Craftsman Independent Union, 1966.

5.   60 LRRM 2222, 59 LRRM 2745, 57 LRRM 2528, 58 LRRM 2344.

6.   *John Wiley & Sons* v. *Livingston,* 376 U.S. 543,555 (1964).

7.   *United Steelworkers* v. *Enterprise Wheel and Car Corp.* 363 U.S. 593,597 (1960).

8.   For these criteria and a full coverage of the subject, see Herbert Schmerty, "When and Where Issue of Arbitrability Can Be Raised." Englewood Cliffs, NJ, Prentice-Hall, Inc., 1966.

9.   For this and other coverage, see "Procedural Arbitrability—A Question for Court or Arbitrators," Labor Law Journal, Dec. 1963, p. 1010.

10.   No. 9 herein.

11.   24 LA 761.

12.   34 LA 617, 33 LA 777, 28 LA 659.

13.   28 LA 321.

14.   46 LA 473.

15.   46 LA 369.

16.   33 LA 130.

17.   33 LA 390.

18. No. 6 herein.
19. 25 LA 39.
20. 1 LA 78.
21. 1 LA 215.
22. 25 LA 50.
23. 21 LA 502.
24. 22 LA 456.
25. Labor Agreement between International Harvester Co. and UAW, 1964.
26. 22 LA 456.
27. 19 LA 737 and also 15 LA 474.
28. Jules Justin. Arbitrability and the Arbitrators Jurisdiction: Mgmt. Rights and the Arbitration Process, BNA, 1956.

4

Selecting the Arbitrator

This is where it all really begins.

A grievance has been processed through the contractual dispute resolution machinery. The parties have met and discussed the issue in the progressive grievance steps stipulated in the contract. Levels of management have met with various officers of the union hierarchy. Viewpoints have been exchanged; arguments have been exchanged and considered by each party. The bargaining history has been explored, witnesses have been heard, records examined, and contract language scrutinized. But the parties still disagree. The next step is the last, an arbitration hearing.

Let us look first at the instrument by which the issue is brought to this binding conclusion.

Contractual Provisions

Here is an example of a typical contractual arbitration provision:

> Arbitration—If the grievance shall not be satisfactorily adjusted through the above steps, the matter may proceed to arbitration, providing the Union notifies the Company of its desire to arbitrate and names its arbitrator within three (3) working days after the date of the regular Union meeting following the Production Manager's reply in Step Three. If the Union fails to notify the Company of its desire to arbitrate within the time stated, the grievance shall be considered dropped.
>
> If the grievance is carried to arbitration as set forth above, the Company shall designate its arbitrator

within five (5) working days or the grievance shall be considered granted.

If the two arbitrators named in the manner set forth above fail to agree on a third arbitrator within fifteen (15) days of the Company's designation either party may request the Director of the Federal Mediation and Conciliation Service to appoint a panel of five (5) impartial, disinterested members. Each party shall have the right to challenge two members of the panel. The remaining member of the panel shall act as the Chairman of the Arbitration Committee. The written decision of the majority of arbitrators shall be final and binding upon both parties. The expenses and compensation incident to the service of the third arbitrator shall be determined in advance and paid jointly by the Company and the Union.[1]

First, the deadline for the union to notify the company of its intent to arbitrate may fluctuate depending upon how close the union's next regularly scheduled meeting is to the third grievance step. Further, the provision requires that the union shall "name its arbitrator" and that the company shall "designate its arbitrator." Presumably, the union and company-appointed "arbitrators" operate as advocates for their respective parties; they are certainly not neutral third parties.

The second paragraph requires the appointed union and company advocates to attempt to agree on an informed, neutral third party, a bona fide arbitrator. Failure to agree is provided for, with selection process devolving on the Federal Mediation and Conciliation Service (FMCS).

This wording could present potential problems. It does not appear to be incumbent on a given party to accept responsibility of making a request to FMCS. What if neither party moved to do so? What if each argued that it was the obligation of the other? Also, no time period is stipulated for forwarding a panel request to FMCS. Problems could result if such panel requests were long delayed—particularly if one party, alleging that the delay of the other was undue, thereby raised a threshold issue of arbitrability, claiming the untimeliness of the request and therefore alleged procedural defectiveness.

This provision does not clearly spell out how the parties shall remove names from the FMCS-submitted panel; it merely says that "each party shall have the right to challenge two members of the panel." Normally, parties alternately remove a name until only one of the initial five remains. It could be inferred that a party could remove any two names it wished, simultaneously. Nor does it indicate which party shall be first to remove a name or names, or how that party is chosen, such as a coin flip.

To suggest that this is nit-picking is not to face industrial realities. The labor-arbitration-research volumes contain hundreds of cases of this type of dispute, which must be decided before arbitration on the actual issue can proceed.

One last point before leaving this provision: It provides that the parties determine in advance the expenses of the arbitrator, which could be interpreted to mean that he should be paid in advance, but the requirement to determine full arbitral costs prior to a hearing is rather unusual and could be difficult.

Let us now look at a contractual provision which is more explicit about the movement of grievances into arbitration and toward the selection of an arbitrator.

> **Step 4: Arbitration.** If no settlement is reached in Step 3 within the specified or agreed time limits, then either party may in writing, within ten work days thereafter request that the matter be submitted to an arbitrator for a prompt hearing as hereinafter provided in 19.6 to 19.9 inclusive.
>
> **Section 19.6. Selection of Arbitrator**—By Agreement. In regard to each case reaching Step 4, the parties will attempt to agree on an arbitrator to hear and decide the particular case. If the parties are unable to agree on an arbitrator within ten work days after submission of the written request for arbitration, the provisions of 19.7 (Selection of Arbitrator—From

Arbitration Panel) shall apply to the selection of an arbitrator.

Section 19.7. Selection of Arbitrator—From Arbitration Panel. Immediately following execution of this Agreement the parties will proceed to compile a list and agree upon a Corporate Panel of five arbitrators. If a case reaches Step 4, and the parties are unable to agree to an arbitrator within the time limit specified in 19.6, the case, irrespective of location, shall be heard and settled by an arbitrator on the Corporate Panel if available. Assignments of cases to arbitrators on the Corporate Panel shall be rotated in the alphabetical order of the last names of those available. An available arbitrator is one who is available to conduct a hearing sixty days (unless mutually extended) after expiration of the time limit specified in 19.6.

Section 19.8. Procedure Where Corporate Panel not Available. In the event, as to any case, that there is no available arbitrator on the Corporate Panel, the parties shall jointly request the American Arbitration Association to submit a panel of seven arbitrators. Such request shall state the general nature of the case and ask that the nominees be qualified to handle the type of case involved. When notification of the names of the seven arbitrators is received, the parties in turn shall have the right to strike a name from the panel until only one name remains. The remaining person shall be the arbitrator. The right to strike the first name from the panel shall be determined by lot.[2]

The draftsmanship here is clearly superior. The language is neither vague nor uncertain. However, even this excellent clause presents one potential problem to the parties— presuming they do not already have an established practice or understanding.

The last sentence reads: "The right to strike the first name from the panel shall be determined by lot." What is "lot?" Presumably, in the context of this agreement, as in countless numbers of labor contracts, the term refers to some type of drawing or other determination by chance. But what type of determination? What if one party perceives this term to mean one kind of contest of chance, while the other considers it something quite different? What if one party is stubborn or irresponsible? What if one party merely wishes to frustrate the orderly processing of the claim to arbitration?

Let us assume that the parties agree to draw straws from a vessel containing straws of various lengths, with the one who draws the longer straw to be considered the winner. Let us further assume that the company representative draws the longer straw. Who strikes the first name from the list of arbiters? The implication of the contractual language could be that the winning party shall strike the first name. But many labor-relations practitioners, representing both labor or management, consider that the party who strikes the first name from an odd-numbered list of arbitrators is at a disadvantage when the list is reduced to only two names. Take a simple example of five names:

Arbitrator A — Company strikes
Arbitrator B — Union strikes
Arbitrator C — Company strikes
Arbitrator D
Arbitrator E

Two names remain, and by virtue of not having struck first, the union has the "final" choice between the two remaining names.

To some, this may seem a small matter; but, to many, it is a matter of great importance. In addition, the bigger the issue to be decided, the more critical the arbitral selection to the parties, and the greater the potential for dispute over who strikes the first name.

Many such problems may be avoided by the use of precise contractual language. In the following example, the provision specifies the party to go first:

The parties shall first attempt to agree upon an impartial arbitrator. If they cannot agree within five (5) working days the parties shall jointly request the Federal Mediation and Conciliation Service to submit a list of

> five (5) names of possible arbitrators. First the Union,
> then the Company, shall alternately strike names from
> the list until only one (1) remains, and this person
> shall act as the arbitrator.[3]

Sometimes it is not specified which party is to strike first in
every instance of arbitral selection. Nevertheless, the contractual provision may enable the parties to reach such
determination:

> 7.02. If the parties cannot agree upon the selection of
> the Arbitrator then the Party demanding arbitration
> shall, within five working days following the above-
> mentioned meeting, upon written notice to the other,
> request the Federal Mediation and Conciliation Service
> (address. . . .) to submit a list of seven (7) qualified
> arbitrators, each of whom must be currently a member
> of National Academy of Arbitrators.

> .03. Within three (3) working days of receipt of said
> list, the Parties will meet, and alternately and in turn
> strike a name until each Party has eliminated a total of
> three (3) names from the list. The Parties shall flip a
> coin to decide which Party strikes the first name and
> the losing party shall strike the first name. Such proce-
> dure shall apply in each case. The Party demanding
> arbitration shall, within two (2) working days there-
> after, with written notice to the other, advise the arbi-
> trator of his selection.[4]

What should be noted first here are the contractual time
limits. Time limitations, particularly ones as brief as these,
enable the parties to move their disputes expeditiously to a
conclusion, and provide one way to remedy delays.

Moreover, in these particular negotiations, representatives of both parties considered it a disadvantage to strike
first, and such is reflected by the contractual language.

Procedures

Arbitrators are selected on either a case-by-case or a permanent basis. Where an arbitrator is chosen for a single case

(the ad hoc method we have been reviewing), a wide variety of procedures have been adopted for determining the impartial umpire. Some parties prefer to leave the selection to an agency such as FMCS or the American Arbitration Association (AAA). While these agencies quite willingly perform such service, they prefer that the parties themselves make the choice.

Another method that has been popular for some years operates as follows: Each party is supplied with a list of names. Each, independently of the other, eliminates from the list names it considers unacceptable to it, for a variety of real or imagined reasons; more often than not, one or more will be acceptable. If two or more names are acceptable, they are numbered in the order of preference. When compared, the lists may look something like this:

Union List	**Company List**
A. Adams	1. A. Adams
5. M. Easy	M. Easy
F. Hard	3. F. Hard
L. Baker	L. Baker
1. S. Smith	5. S. Smith
W. Jones	W. Jones
2. H. White	2. H. White
4. C. Black	C. Black
3. B. Brown	4. B. Brown

Only H. White, S. Smith, and B. Brown are acceptable to both parties. Adding the ratings, H. White would be first choice, having received the lowest numerical total ($2 + 2 = 4$), with S. Smith in second place ($1 + 5 = 6$), and B. Brown in third place ($3 + 4 = 7$). The lower the total score of the arbitral candidate, the higher his level of acceptability to both parties, since each party has numbered the candidates in the order of its preference, beginning with 1. Thus the appointment as arbitrator would first be offered to White; if he declined or was unable to serve, the parties would offer the post first to Smith and then to Brown.

Obviously, there are shortcomings in this system, as in the others. By alternately striking names from a preestab-

lished list provided by those agencies, the parties are more
or less stuck with their own selection. Of course, such lists
may by mutual agreement of the parties, be returned to the
agencies, if all names are wholly unacceptable to both
parties. However, this is relatively rare, primarily because
of the care of FMCS and AAA in constructing arbitration
panels.

In this procedure, there is always a good chance that
the parties will each strike all the names that are acceptable
to the other, which would necessitate a second list and a
repetition of the process, imposing lengthy delays upon the
selection of an arbitrator. Also, in theory at least, it could
happen over and over. The answer may lie in the parties
agreeing to limit themselves to a maximum number of exclusions, say three names each from a panel of seven.

The parties may also elect to set up permanent machinery for resolving disputes. An example of one such arrangement follows:

> Within thirty (30) days after the date of this Agree-
> ment, representatives of the parties hereto will obtain
> from the American Arbitration Association a list of Ar-
> bitrators, and will agree upon a panel of three arbitra-
> tors, obtaining additional lists, if necessary. The parties
> shall furnish said Association the names of the arbitra-
> tors so selected. Thereafter the Association shall desig-
> nate one of said arbitrators to hear each grievance that
> may be referred to arbitration but no one arbitrator
> shall hear more than three grievances. If said panel
> shall be exhausted, representatives of the parties shall
> in the same manner select a second panel of arbitrators
> to hear grievances arising thereafter, each of whom
> may hear not more than three grievances.[5]

Systems providing for permanent arbitrators are more frequently found in large enterprises with long collective bargaining histories and a large number of cases going into
arbitration.

Several arguments are put forward for permanent-arbitrator systems: A permanent arbitrator comes to know the

pecularities of the business better; he understands the features of the relationship which makes it unique to the given parties; his rulings have conformity, continuity, and uniformity, which simplifies enforcement of the contract; and his awards set precedents that form guidelines supplementing the contract and smoothing labor relations.

However, the permanent-arbitrator system is not without its opponents. Labor relations practitioners may contend that: The arbitrator tends too often to play the role of mediator; he eventually tends to supplant management in the determination of industrial relations policies; he may, because he comes to feel that he should please both sides, have a tendency to decide the issue on the basis of the trend of decisions instead of on the merits of each particular case; and his presence may promote the number of grievances pushed into arbitration.

In securing a permanent arbitrator, one should:

(1) Be extremely thorough in researching and selecting the individual who will serve. It is easier and less painful to avoid a mistake than to undo one.

(2) Use ad hoc arbitration at least until you are quite familiar with the process, and how various arbitrators function during hearings. Exposure to different arbitrators may be helpful later in the selection of a permanent arbitrator.

(3) Have a clear understanding of fee arrangements with the permanent umpire selected. What are the arbitrator's charges? How available is he? Will he readily give his time without unreasonable delay? If a yearly retainer is required, how frequent were arbitral cases in the past? These are a few of the primary questions that must be answered satisfactorily.

(4) Even if a permanent arbitrator is decided upon, consider providing in the labor agreement for selection and use of temporary arbitrators when the office of the permanent umpire is vacant or when for any reason he cannot serve. It is much

>better to take this precaution before an emer-
>gency occurs than to try to cope with it just
>when the need for arbitral help is greatest.

(5) In a multiplant, or multidivision, operation, consider using the same permanent individual under
each of several agreements. If the industry has an
employers' association, consider joining with
others to select and retain a single umpire, especially if each member of the group feels the need
for an arbitrator who understands the peculiarities
of the industry. A wgroup may be able to attract and
finance an arbitrator of wider experience and national reputation. When such arrangements are
made, the parties often name several alternates
rather than a single permanent selection.

There are other reasons why careful selection of a permanent arbitrator is so important. An arbitrator conducts a
hearing in a manner peculiar to his own philosophy and
personality: He may run a tight or loose hearing. He may
accept objections raised against testimony or procedure,
disallow them or "take it for whatever it may later prove to
be worth." He may be a strict constructionist in his interpretation of the agreement, ignoring any factors outside of
contract language. Or he may give weight to the customs
and practices of the parties, previous arbitration decisions,
previous grievance settlements, and the history of collective
bargaining discussions between the parties.

Such matters should certainly be considered in selecting any arbitrator, whether for permanent duty or for ad hoc
service.

Arbitration may be conducted either by a single nonpartisan arbitrator or a tripartite board, composed of an
equal number of employer and union representatives and an
impartial member acting as chairman; a few agreements
allow the parties the option of either individual or board.
Under some contracts, the partisan representatives first attempt to settle the dispute. Only after they have been
unable to agree is the impartial arbitrator added to make a

decision possible. Most often, all members of an arbitration board, including the impartial chairman, are selected before the arbitration hearings start.

Agreements calling for permanent arbitration usually specify a single arbitrator, rather than a tripartite board. Sometimes only the impartial chairman serves on a permanent basis, with company and union representatives selected for each dispute.

Whatever the procedure prescribed, only the requirements of the labor contract limit the selection of an arbitrator. Unless the contract specifies that the arbitrator chosen must come from panels of FMCS or AAA, or be a member of the National Academy, the company and union may choose anyone they wish to arbitrate for them, and they often obtain their third-party neutral from other sources. It is not unheard of for a priest, minister, rabbi, mayor or other public official – even a governor – to decide a labor issue. Parties may even agree upon an apparently partisan person.

But the quality of the arbitrator may eventually prove to be as significant as the merits of the case and the quality of presentation at the arbitral hearing.

CITATIONS

1. Labor Agreement between Englehard Minerals and Chemicals Corporation and Local 238, United Cement, Lime and Gypsum Workers, International Union, Gardner, GA, 1972.

2. Labor Agreement between the Boeing Company and International Association of Machinists, effective 12/12/71.

3. Labor Agreement between McDonnell Douglas Corporation and IAM, 1972.

4. Sherwood Medical Industries, Inc., and Dist. 50, UMW, 1969.

5. Labor Agreement between American Enka Corporation and United Textile Workers of America, 1969.

5

Researching the Arbitrator

We are now ready for the next step.

The Federal Mediation and Conciliation Service (FMCS), the American Arbitration Association (AAA), or another source has submitted a list of names of arbitrators to each party. The list contains an odd number of names, usually five or seven.

The list lies before you on your desk. If you are lucky, one or two of the names are familiar. You may have previously used some of the arbitrators listed and thus may already be familiar with their style, and how they conduct hearings. You have also developed a system for arriving at conclusions.

If so, you have somewhat minimized the research chore of sifting through the potential arbiters. Those who go to arbitration often, or fairly often, have an edge in their familiarity with the professionals in the business of deciding disputes as neutral third parties.

Because they have appeared on previous lists, you may have some knowledge of the background, experience, qualifications, and general reputation of certain names. Presumably, they may have been checked out in the past. If so, your chore is further diminished and one-fifth or one-seventh or more of the basic questions have already been answered.

But if all the names are unfamiliar, what then? Or worse yet, if you don't know what steps to take to determine the arbitrator's qualifications, what then?

Qualifications

Among the qualities of character—as opposed to expertise—the parties are entitled to find in their selection, none
is more important than impartiality.

Everyone is possessed of certain biases and prejudices
on an endless variety of matters. At the same time, it is not
unreasonable to expect that an individual will discipline
himself to decide the issues on their own merits. Sentiment
or bias for or against an issue, a particular party, or the
conditions of the labor agreement are factors that must be
divorced from the decision-making process. From the opening of the hearing until a decision is rendered, an open mind
is not merely desirable, it is essential, not only to provide
equity and impartial justice to the parties and their relationship, but also for the preservation of an honorable arbitration profession.

The absence of these essential qualities is definitely the
exception; that is why arbitration and its neutral professionals have flourished for so many years. Without these qualities of character, practicing arbitrators, and the process they
serve, would never have endured. At the same time, the
arbitrator must exercise his own best judgment, which
sometimes results in an unpopular decision. If such an
award is the result of sound judgment, not of partiality or
favoritism, the arbitrator has provided a valuable service. An
arbitrator is not engaged in a popularity contest. Accordingly, while one or both parties may be displeased with a
particular decision, they will not lose faith in the fundamental benefits of the process so long as they are convinced that
awards result from judgment impartially exercised.

The integrity of the arbitrator is equally important. The
arbitrator does not seek to serve the parties; nor is he
elected to the position he holds. As a consequence, he does
not serve at the sufferance of either party. He has not, nor
should he have, any vested interest in, or allegiance to,
representatives of either faction. His integrity has been established through his prior business and personal dealings
and affiliations.

To many labor-relations practitioners, the fact that an arbitrator has considerable previous experience in representing either labor or management exclusively gives the kiss of death to his serving as a neutral. However, previous partisan service does not necessarily render an individual incapable of impartiality and integrity. In this respect, labor arbitration is somewhat like other fields of endeavor. Many excellent defense lawyers were previously district attorneys. Many referees with unquestioned integrity were formerly players; some even performed for the same teams they later render judgments on. A more reliable determinant of whether the arbitrator's feelings of partisanship still prevail would be the cases he has decided and how he has decided them. Prior partisanship may have been the very source of the depth and breadth of insight and experience that enables him to appraise the issues and circumstances with greater understanding. Some of the ablest and most informed neutrals practicing as labor arbitrators today, with impeccable reputations, came either from the labor movement, or from management.

Whether certain experience, education, or training is necessary for all arbitrators is questionable. No two possess exactly the same background attributes; most possess the essential qualifies of character which enable them to render decisions impartially and to serve with unchallengeable integrity. But with regard to actual experience and qualifications, there are a few helpful indications.

If the individual is a member of the National Academy of Arbitrators, he is an experienced neutral who has met several high standards imposed by his own peers. If he has passed the scrutiny of the membership committee of the Academy, the odds are substantially good that the arbitrator will possess the desired credentials.

The Academy, however, does not include all those who have impressive qualifications and capabilities as arbitrators. The Academy, founded in 1947, takes in relatively few new members each year, so that absence from its roster does not necessarily indicate a lack of ability or proficiency. The

FMCS and AAA also investigate arbitrators on their panels. In fact, both agencies require that the individual provide a number of references to acceptability, knowledge, and character from the ranks of *both* labor and management. In addition, he must demonstrate sufficient labor-management exposure to qualify him for consideration. The rules of nonpartisan arbitration agencies forbid an arbitrator to serve in a case in which he has any financial or personal interest or is related to any of the parties, unless the parties waive this condition in writing.

The qualification of arbitrators is doubly important because they have been deemed to be judicial officers with some immunities from suit by parties, since arbitrators "must be free from the fear of reprisals" and "must of necessity be uninfluenced by any fear of consequences for their acts."[1]

The foundation stone of successful arbitration is the confidence of the parties in the fairness and competence of the arbitrator.[2] Yet disparaging remarks about the integrity, principles, and biases of arbitrators often contribute to the unusually troublesome problem of selecting an arbitrator. The usefulness of arbitration in the field of industrial relations is largely the result of the quality of the arbitrators, their personal and professional integrity, their intimate acquaintance with the varied facets of industrial life, and their judgment. The parties themselves are mostly responsible for whatever undermining of arbitration there has been. In their eagerness to win cases, they contribute materially to reducing the usefulness of arbitration and to breeding attitudes of cynicism about arbitration on the part of companies, union, and the public generally. An agreement between New Jersey Bell Telephone Company and the Electrical Workers (IBEW) contained this clause among its arbitration provisions:

(3) At the same time that written demand for arbitration is served upon the other party, the American Arbitration Association shall be requested in writing to appoint an impartial chairman. The Impartial shall not

> be an officer, director, or employee of the company or
> of any company in the Bell System, nor shall he be a
> member, officer, official, employee, representative, at-
> torney or counsel of the Union or of any other Union
> of labor organization.

It is doubtful that such a restriction need be spelled out in
the labor agreement. It is not conceivable that AAA would
knowingly submit a panel containing the names of persons
from the contractually prohibited categories. More often,
the parties specify in their contract the desired rather than
the unacceptable qualities sought in the arbitrator. For
example:

> Within two (2) working days thereafter, the Parties
> shall jointly write to the Arbitrator selected and re-
> quest hearing dates. Neither party shall deliberately
> delay the setting of a hearing date.
>
> 1. Such arbitrators must be technically qualified to
>   resolve disputes and have skill, knowledge, and/or
>   experience relating to measurements of standards
>   of work.
>
> 2. Such arbitrators must have prior arbitration expe-
>   rience in regularly deciding issues relating to mea-
>   surements of standards of work.
>
> 3. Any arbitrator selected by the above procedures
>   must be currently a member of the National Acad-
>   emy of Arbitrators.[3]

This contract contains two grievance and arbitration provisions, one dealing with disputes outside the "wage incentive plan," and the other, quoted in part, dealing with
disputes about the administration and implementation of an
incentive standards program, and specifying arbitrators
who have industrial engineering expertise, education, and/
or experience.

Relatively few contracts specify qualifications for arbitrators, except when technically trained and experienced
persons are sought in disputes involving time-study and
incentive systems. Appointment of public officeholders is

occasionally prohibited and lawyers may be precluded from serving as partisan arbitrators. Persons living within a specified distance from the enterprise may be declared ineligible for service as arbitrators; on the other hand, a person familiar with the particular industry may be specified.

Substantial arbitration experience is obviously of considerable benefit, both to the arbitrator and to the parties he serves. However, the absence of experience as an arbitrator can be materially compensated for by a keen and analytical mind with the capability to quickly grasp new subject matter. Where parties have adequately prepared and intelligently presented the facts, competence may be acquired during the course of hearings. Of course, when the least question arises about integrity, the arbitrator's usefulness ceases. This ingredient is the equal of maturity or judgment; all are indispensable. Special knowledge about the matter to be decided is rarely required. In the vast majority of cases, general experience in industrial matters, however obtained, will enable an arbitrator to relate to the issues at hand.

Does an arbitrator need legal training? The answer is no. It is true that many arbitrators have been trained in law, as have many labor relations practitioners. It is also true that training in legal affairs provides a discipline that promotes objective and analytical thinking. It teaches the evaluation of facts and information, with limitations on personal prejudice. It tends to eliminate extraneous matters and considers pertinent factors only. While several of the ablest established arbitrators have law backgrounds, many equally able and established arbitrators do not.

It also has to be recognized that not all legally trained individuals make good arbitrators. The arbitrator's legal background may, in some circumstances, even be a hindrance to a full and open hearing. Because the arbitration process is only quasi-judicial, strict rules of evidence, testimony, and procedure do not apply. One of the virtues of the process is its speed and simplicity. Introduction of "legalese" into the system may complicate it unduly. It may stifle both the informal presentations of cases and dispositions toward subsequent use of the process. How someone reasons and exercises good judgment, how he analyzes situations, and how much objectivity he demonstrates are far more important considerations than the formal education he may have.

Evaluation of Arbitral Candidates

The Bureau of National Affairs publishes *Labor Arbitration Reports,* which provide accurate and authoritative information about arbitration awards, and also information about particular arbitrators, including their names, addresses, telephone numbers, birth dates, training, positions, affiliations, and publications. These volumes and similar reports are invaluable.

One word of caution is in order. Only a very small percentage of all decisions are published. Nor are all decisions of any particular arbitrator published. Arbitrators choose cases to submit to the publishing services, which then make a further selection. Moreover, the parties must grant permission for publication. The great majority of cases never get into print. Nevertheless, a significant number are available to the interested and diligent researcher.

The increase in both number and significance of arbitration awards has led BNA to segregate the text of court decisions into separate volumes, leaving room in *Labor Arbitration Reports* for increased coverage of labor arbitration awards. These reports, with their Index-Digest, contain the "Directory of Arbitrators." The reports also list the unions involved in the reported cases, by popular name and the official name of the national or international union and its subordinate branches.

Consulting these publications is essential to a thorough and comprehensive job of research, but there are other equally productive sources. Additional information may also be obtained from Prentice-Hall's *Who's Who* (of arbitrators), which gives age, address, education, occupation, affiliations, experience, publications (often insightful as to labor-relations philosophy), awards published, and a variety of other miscellaneous information.

The Commerce Clearing House volumes, *American Labor Arbitration Awards* (ALAA), report comprehensively on hundreds of awards. Some cases published by CCH may also be found in BNA's *Labor Arbitration Reports,* but there are many reported by one which are not published by the other. Both services are equally impressive; if both are available, the dedicated researcher may find it is worthwhile to compare the reported cases that pertain to a particular arbitral candidate.

The panels maintained by AAA and FMCS contain the names of hundreds of qualified arbitrators. Their responses to requests for panels also include pertinent biographical data, as for instance, using the FMCS format:

Harold Decisive

Occupation: Professor Economics and Chairman, Department of Economics

Address: (Bus)   Ohio State University
                 Columbus, Ohio

         (Res)   1050 Treelined Street
                 Columbus, Ohio

Telephone: West 6-7689   East 2-3804

Arbitration experience: Arbitrator since 1962. Majority of working time devoted to teaching, with balance spent in arbitration. Has experience in arbitration of wages, fringe benefits, grievances concerning management prerogatives, overtime and premium pay, job specifications, seniority, discipline and discharge.

Other experience: Fourteen years teaching experience. Labor relations consultant, Atomic Energy Commission, 1964–1967. Mediator, U.S. Conciliation Service, 1955–1957. Corps of Engineers, U.S. Army, 1952–55.

> Professional affiliations: Arbitration Association, Industrial Relations Research Association, American Economics Association.
>
> Education: B.A., M.A., Ph.D.
>
> Date of Birth: March 6, 1922.
>
> Per diem fee: Not exceeding $150.

While they are helpful and informative in themselves, the data sheets should only be the basis for further investigation, not final determination. In addition to checking the BNA and CCH reports, you may wish to ask AAA or FMCS for the names of parties to proceedings before a given arbitrator. Employer associations and chambers of commerce, too, can sometimes furnish lists of cases decided by local arbitrators. "Repeat orders" from the same parties are a particularly strong endorsement.

As many as possible of those who have advocated cases before a candidate should be contacted. Try to pin them down to specific good or bad qualities—remembering, nevertheless, that anyone who has lost a case may be inclined to blame the arbitrator. On the other hand, a recommendation from the losing party or a criticism from the party given the award should have special weight.

Of the many questions that may be raised with parties who have already had experience with a candidate, the following are among the more pertinent:

- What was the issue decided?
- Did the arbitrator consider only the relevant contractual provision, or did he give weight to such other matters as the practices and customs of the parties, and the history of collective bargaining on the disputed clauses?
- Did the arbitrator use a transcript of the hearing by a court stenographer, or did he make his own notes?
- How did he conduct the hearing? Was it informal or legalistic?

- Did he rule on objections, or did he accept all evidence proffered by the parties?

- Did he ask many questions—or did he simply accept what was given him?

- How soon after the close of the hearing was the award submitted? If not within the preferred 30 days, was there a justifiable reason for delay?

- Were his opinion and award clear and understandable?

- In the opinion, were his remarks on point with the issue to be decided, or did he delve into extraneous matters?

- Were his charges reasonable in light of the length of the hearing(s) and the complexity of the case?

The reason for most of these questions is fairly evident. They deal with the promptness, style, objectivity, analytical ability, rationale, and fees—all important considerations. The information may give one party a decided edge: It may influence the approach to be taken and style to be followed. The party may be able to prepare its witnesses better. One arbitrator may be more expensive than planned for, although other positive determinations may outweigh this factor. The discovery that an arbitrator is inclined to go far afield, even when he renders a favorable award, may hint at the possibility of winning the battle, but losing the war. And a candidate rejected for one case may still be acceptable for a later case. After the prospective client has talked with other parties and read opinions, he should judge the arbitrator on the general quality of his work, not on how many cases he has decided for one side or the other. If the majority of his awards favor the union, this does not necessarily indicate a prounion bias, since a great many variables enter the picture.

Whatever the findings, they should not be disposed of. Instead, an arbitration file should be used to accumulate information pertinent to the selection and evaluation of arbitrators. Some names will appear time and again on lists.

And if you want others in the labor-management community to share opinions with you, you must reciprocate. Any party who has cause to be dissatisfied with a particular arbitrator should share his concern fairly and objectively with the agency who provided the name. The agency will be grateful for constructive criticism. An appraisable pattern of comments from different parties will enable it to determine if reaction is necessary. Preserving the results of research can save you considerable time, trouble, and expense later.

CITATIONS

1. 26 LA 122.
2. Stein, Emanuel. "Problem Areas in Labor Arbitration," New York University Third Annual Conference on Labor, pp. 267–86, Albany, NY, Mathew Bender & Co., 1950.
3. Labor Agreement between Brunswick Corporation and UBCJA, Local 824, 1972.

6

Preparing Your Case for Arbitration

Thorough preparation of cases for arbitration is of paramount importance. Ordinarily the arbitrator can only understand the case from evidence and arguments presented at the arbitration hearing. You must fully understand your own case in order to communicate it effectively to the arbitrator, and full understanding depends upon thorough preparation.

In some cases the emphasis is on the facts; each party will concentrate upon proving, largely through testimony of witnesses, that the facts are as that party sees them. In other cases the facts may be less important or not disputed, the controversy centering perhaps upon the proper interpretation of the collective agreement. In still other cases, economic and statistical data may be especially important.

Thus, the nature of the case should be considered in determining which items of the following "preparation" check list should be emphasized. No significance lies in the order in which they are listed:

1. Review the history of the case as developed at the prearbitral steps of the grievance procedure.

2. Study the entire agreement to ascertain all clauses bearing directly or indirectly on the dispute. Also, compare current provisions with previous versions; language changes might be significant.

3. Examine the instruments used to initiate the arbitration to determine the general authority of the

arbitrator, and thus the scope of the arbitration.

4. Talk to *everyone* (even those the other party might use as witnesses) who might be able to help you develop a full picture of the case from different viewpoints. You will better understand not only your own case but also your opponent's; if you can anticipate your opponent's case, you can better prepare to rebut it.

5. Interview your own witnesses (1) to determine what each knows about the case; (2) to make certain they understand the relation of their testimony to the whole case; and (3) to check their testimony and acquaint them with the process of cross-examination. Summarize in writing the expected testimony of each witness for review as the witness testifies to ensure that no important points are overlooked. Many parties outline in advance the questions to be asked each witness.

6. Examine all documents that might be relevant to the case. Organize those you expect to use and make copies for the arbitrator and the other party. If needed documents are in the exclusive possession of the other party, ask that they be made available before (preferably) or at the hearing.

7. Visit the physical premises involved in the dispute to better visualize what occurred. Also, consider asking at the hearing that the arbitrator (accompanied by both parties) also visit the site.

8. Consider pictorial or statistical exhibits. If the matter is appropriate, one exhibit can be more effective than many words. However, exhibits which do not "fit" the case, or are inaccurate or misleading, are almost certain to be damaging to their proponent.

9. Consider what the parties' past practice has been in comparable situations.

10. Attempt to determine whether there is some "key" point upon which the case might turn. If so, you may wish to concentrate upon that point.

11. In interpretation cases, prepare a written argument to support your interpretation.

12. Research prior arbitration awards between the parties and the published awards of other parties on the subject in dispute to see how similar issues have been approached in other cases.

13. Outline your case and discuss it with other persons in your group. This will strengthen your case by uncovering matters that need further attention. Then, too, it will tend to underscore policy and strategy considerations that may be very important. Use of the outline at the hearing will facilitate an organized presentation.

Thorough preparation requires ingenuity to illuminate all the possibilities of the case. Certainly, the arbitrator needs a full picture of the case to reach a sound decision.

The most successful advocates prepare their cases themselves. If they cannot prepare every aspect personally, they will direct every step, interview the witnesses, study every document, read every relevant case, and in every way gain first-hand knowledge and complete mastery of the facts and the law of the case. Certainly, until the advocate can afford excellent assistants on whose preparation he can rely, he should prepare the case himself from beginning to end. Not only will the mastery of the case improve his chances of success, but the insight he will gain into the practical problems of preparation will give him the ability to guide preparation by others later. The advocate who starts his career with small cases which he thinks are not worth thorough preparation is not likely to get more important cases. On the other hand the advocate who prepares his minor cases thoroughly will not only win more cases, and thereby attract more favorable attention, but will also acquire the experience and confidence to succeed with the more important cases that are likely to follow.

Start preparing the case as soon as the grievance is filed. Every grievance filed should be treated from the outset as though it were destined for arbitration. In fact, if all grievances were handled that carefully, many fewer would actually have to go the full route. It might also be surprising to see how many which go the ultimate distance are found in favor of the more diligent party.

There is serious danger in postponing the preparation of a case until shortly before the hearing. Not only should all the facts be checked, but all the available evidence should be in the hands of the advocate at the earliest possible date, to protect against possible loss of valuable evidence, and prevent the advocate from going off in the wrong direction in his theory of the action or of the defense. Incorrect or incomplete evidence at the hearing can be seriously damaging. Even if it can be amended, a competent opponent will find opportunity to point out its insufficiency or the shifting in your position. Too, careless or uninformed questioning of witnesses, can lead to disaster even when an advocate, though careless, is otherwise able and intelligent.

Preliminary Interview of Witnesses

Of first importance in any action are the facts—the exact facts, and all the facts. As you prepare, let the witness tell his own story. If you shut him off and insist on getting only answers to specific questions, you may screen out some important point, for you cannot possibly anticipate all the facts in every case. After getting his story, you will then have to ask questions to sift the relevant aspects, to emphasize salient features, to fill in gaps, and to help the witness see the outline of the total case, as you develop it from the facts before you. If the witness can understand your theory of the case, he may tell you facts which he otherwise might have inadvertently overlooked or consciously and erroneously discarded as immaterial. In other words, you must get your witness to give you assistance which is valuable because it is intelligent.

In questioning the witness you must be a friendly but nonetheless searching cross-examiner. It is your task to learn all the bad as well as all the good points of the case, to marshal the evidence intelligently, prepare arguments properly, and avoid unpleasant surprises at the hearing. Advance knowledge may enable you to weaken the effect of your adversary's cross-examination by explaining or minimizing unfavorable facts or neutralize some of his direct evidence by anticipating it in your own direct examination.

A witness in arbitral litigation can hardly be objective about his case. Consciously or otherwise, the good points will be exaggerated, the bad minimized. Self-interest or bias may lead to fabrication or omission; faulty observation or poor memory, to distortion and confusion. Infrequently there may even be a deliberate or psychopathic invention of a story which has little or no foundation in fact. Early investigation will save an advocate a great deal of woe in some cases.

Experienced advocates have learned that though an honest and rational witness will not invent facts, he may suppress them. Simplest to cope with is unconscious suppression, caused by a lack of understanding as to what is important. You can generally overcome this type of suppression by detailed questioning of the witness. Somewhat more elusive is subsconscious suppression, psychologically induced by the wish to put one's best foot forward, or by nature's trick of inducing forgetfulness of what one does not like to remember. This type of suppression may also be overcome by detailed questioning, but it must be handled more delicately than the first type and requires a keen observation of psychological reactions. While some persons are better natural psychologists than others, every trial advocate can benefit from the study of practical psychology.

In any case, you must find a way to make your witness realize how important it is that he confide in you so that you will not be faced with any surprises at the trial. A fact is much more damaging if it catches you by surprise. Knowing about a damaging fact in advance, you may be able to explain it and take the sting out.

Not only must the witness be frank with you; you must be frank with the witness. Some advocates assume an optimistic attitude, apparently intended to encourage his party and its witnesses in the early stages of the case. There is danger, however, in too much optimism. An objective recognition of the problems involved in the litigation is not only the ethical approach but is also, in the long run, the best insurance against disappointments and dissatisfaction for your party. Any weaknesses in a case should be discussed candidly so that the client will understand the difficulties. Sometimes this understanding will increase their helpfulness in the preparation of the case. At other times they may be brought to recognize the advisability of a compromise settlement. Furthermore, if the case should go to an arbitral hearing and be lost because weaknesses were glossed over, the failure will seem incompatible with any earlier enthusiasm and optimism of the advocate.

Some advocates fail to take detailed notes. They either make a few cryptic notations, understood only by themselves, or depend entirely on their memories. This is dangerous and unwise. No advocate has a memory good enough to guarantee recall of all the necessary details at the right moment. Moreover, it is useful to preserve an accurate record of the facts while they are fresh in the minds of the witnesses. Then, too, the person who confers on the case at the outset may not be available later. The records in the file should, therefore, always be in such condition that any advocate called into the case on short notice by studying the file can understand the case quickly and fully.

All witnesses should be interviewed as early as possible. Begin by asking the witness how he happened to know what he relates. If he says he was a witness, find out where he came from, where he was going, what he was doing at the moment of the occurrence, and exactly where he was with respect to what he says he saw or heard. It is also important to ascertain whether there were any intervening objects, stationary or moving, so that you may determine whether he could have actually seen or heard what he says he saw or heard.

Sometimes it may be important to obtain a signed statement from the witness. If the witness prepares the statement in his own handwriting, he will be unlikely to repudiate it. If it is not in his handwriting, have him sign a statement that he has read each page signed or initialed by him, and the facts it reports are true.

The importance of obtaining such statements in certain cases cannot be overemphasized. An employee may leave or be discharged before the hearing. He may lose interest, or become hostile. He may be too concerned about his new job to go to the arbitral hearing willingly. A friend today may become a foe tomorrow. A witness who evidences interest at the time an event occurs may sometimes lose interest later.

Final preparation for the hearing should include a review of all documentary evidence in the case—not only those exhibits which you intend to offer in evidence but also those which the opposing party may offer. The exhibits should be arranged for ready use at the hearing. And you will need three copies of each at the hearing—one for the arbitrator, one for the opposing party, and one for yourself.

If there are only a few exhibits, they may be arranged in a folder in the order in which you expect to use them at the trial. Another folder should hold correspondence and other documents which you do not intend to use but for which a need may arise at the trial. If they are not too numerous, the simplest arrangement is to keep these documents in chronological order.

It may sometimes be helpful to prepare special exhibits. It may be desirable, for instance, to enlarge photographs. In a case which involves extensive testimony by accountants based on voluminous records, the accountant should prepare such visual aids as balance sheets, operating statements, comparative statements and summaries as exhibits.

Complicated cases need, and those of substantial importance deserve, even more detailed preparation.

Final Interview of Witnesses

No matter how careful the preliminary preparation, the careful advocate will not go to trial without final interviews with all the witnesses who are available to him, to preview the facts to which each will testify on direct examination, or about which he may be asked on cross-examination.

After the final interview, after the facts have been reviewed, the witness should be questioned just as you expect to ask the questions at the hearing. Simulate your hearing-room manner as much as possible, so that the witness may feel more at ease during the actual procedings.

The witness should be familiarized with any exhibits which he will have to identify, interpret, or testify about. Tell him what the hearing-room is like. Tell him when each exhibit will be introduced, and why, so that he can understand the importance of each as a link in the chain.

But letting a witness memorize his testimony is a horrible mistake. If memory falters, the witness may "collapse." Memorized testimony can often be detected and the fact that the story may be true in all particulars will be crushed. Furthermore, if all witnesses use the same language, the arbitrator naturally will be suspicious, no matter how truthful the witnesses are.

The witness should be aware that what is important is the substance of his testimony rather than the exact language, except where the exact wording of an alleged abusive, threatening or slanderous remark, or the like, is vital to the case. He should understand the aim of the examiner, the purpose of the questions, and the nature of the answer which each of the questions seeks to elicit. He will not only be a more intelligent and cooperative witness, but also a more effective one, if he knows what he is talking about.

After you and the witness have gone over his direct testimony, assume the role of opposing counsel, in order to accustom him to cross-examination by your opponent. If you know the style of your opponent, imitate him as closely as possible. If you cross-examine in a mild manner, the witness may receive a disconcerting shock if at the hearing the cross-examiner shouts or bullies, uses a sarcastic tone, or otherwise attempts to discomfit the witness.

You cannot possibly conceive of every question that your opponent will ask, but you can anticipate some of the important ones if you train yourself to be critical of your own case. If you are sufficiently objective, you will find the weaknesses and omissions in the story told by the witness, and you will concentrate on those weaknesses in your "cross-examination."

Prepare also to deal with the weaknesses of the witness as distinguished from the weaknesses of the testimony. Does he have a pecuniary interest of the witness in the case? A friendship for another party? A bias? What is the nature of his position? Is there any other factor which may influence his testimony? If the witness has something in his background which may be subject to attack, you cannot afford to spare his feelings in your office and then subject him, without preparation, to a far less friendly probing at the hearing. You must go over the facts so that the witness will not, under the influence of shock, excitement, or embarrassment during the hearing, suppress a truth to "protect himself," and ruin his own credibility and your chances of success. You must impress upon him the importance of his telling you the truth so that you can make the effect of any attack milder by preparing for it. The material below, directed to witnesses, should be helpful.

Instructions for Witnesses

Being a witness in an arbitration proceedings is not a comfortable experience. You are understandably worried about your testimony. You want to leave a favorable impression. You naturally are concerned that during cross-examination the opposing advocate will attempt to discredit your testimony, to cause you to contradict yourself and thereby sound inconsistent and untruthful.

It is important to be as comfortable as possible, to be aware of how arbitral proceedings are conducted, to know what to expect and how to comport yourself. Equally as important, you should be able to give your evidence in such a manner that the arbitrator understands and believes it. The following will help you:

1. *Do sit erect and comfortable.*
   How you sit in the witness chair can influence the arbitrator's perceptions of your credibility. Sit comfortably erect. Try not to slouch, change position frequently, fidget, or wave your arms about. Your objective is to appear cool, calm, confident, self-assured.

2. *Do tell the truth.*
   Tell the truth on the witness stand. Also, tell the truth—all of it, not just some of it, or most of it, but all you know about the case, good and bad—to your advocate when he's preparing the case for trial.

3. *Don't volunteer information.*
   Answer the opposing advocate's questions honestly and directly, but answer only what he asks. If you can answer with a yes or a no, do so—and stop. If there is something you've left untold which could be helpful to your case, it is the responsibility of your advocate to bring it out during re-direct examination. Remember, you are not on the witness stand to try the case. You are there only to answer the questions asked of you.

4. *Do answer all questions asked of you, no matter by whom, in a courteous and forthright manner.*
   Your own advocate will ask you questions, the other advocate will examine you, and the arbitrator may also ask you questions. Answer them all in the same tone, in the same manner, with the same demeanor—honestly, forthrightly, courteously. Don't use a different manner or tone with one than you do with another.

5. *Don't argue with the opposing advocate—or the arbitrator.*
   It is the legitimate job of the other party's advocate to try to upset you, get you angry or irritated,

attempt to discredit you, and cause you to contradict yourself. He may use harsh tactics or an aggressive manner. But don't play into his hands.
Don't get angry, sarcastic, smart-alecky, pugna-
cious, or in any other way emotional. Remember,
you're not responsible for his behavior—you're
only accountable for your own.

6. *Do be alert and attentive.*
   If you are in the hearing room during other testimony, listen attentively. If other evidence reminds
   you of something relevant you forgot to mention
   to your advocate, quietly pass down a note telling
   him of it.

7. *Do watch the arbitrator.*
   The arbitrator's body language may communicate
   his attitude. Watch when he picks up his pencil to
   make a note. Has something significant just happened? Was it something helpful to your case? Or
   something damaging? If the former, you may realize an opportunity to beef-up a strong point favorable to your side; if the latter, you may realize a
   need to shore-up against a weakness in your case.
   Quietly pass a note to your advocate of what
   you've observed.

8. *Don't patronize the arbitrator.*
   Be courteous and polite in your reactions to the
   arbitrator. If you treat him in an exceptionally
   friendly manner, and the other party observes it,
   the arbitrator is placed in an awkward position.
   Being human, he may feel he must compensate
   for this by demonstrating to the other party that
   he has not been prejudiced by your actions or
   words.

9. *Do consider each question before answering.*
   Questions should be answered without hesitation,
   long pauses, or undue reflection. But don't let the
   cross-examiner set the pace for your answers. He
   may fire questions at you rapidly to cause you to
   answer without due reflection. Think before you
   answer.

10. *Don't be afraid to say "I don't know."*
    No witness is expected to know all there is to
    know about any given subject. Don't offer opin-
    ions or conjecture when you don't know the spe-
    cific answer. If you have answered other questions
    asked of you straightforwardly, giving specific
    answers, you will actually enhance your credibility
    on those matters when you say "I don't know" to
    other questions.

11. *Don't answer a question you don't understand.*
    If a question is ambiguous or unclear to you, ask
    the questioner to repeat the question, or rephrase
    it. Do this as many times as necessary for you to
    clearly comprehend the question. The question
    may have been deliberately phrased to be suscep-
    tible to more than one interpretation. You may be
    mistaken in your interpretation of what the ques-
    tion is asking. If you answer without being certain
    what is being asked, your interpretation may differ
    from the arbitrator, who thus may misunderstand
    your answer.

12. *Don't deny you've reviewed your testimony with
    your advocate.*
    Occasionally the other party's advocate may ask
    you if you've gone over your testimony with your
    advocate prior to the arbitration hearing, implying
    that this is wrong. Tell the truth. If the answer is
    yes—and rarely will it be otherwise—say so. The
    practice is routine. The arbitrator will assume that
    you have, and it will reflect negatively on your
    credibility if you deny it. Tell the truth on this and
    in all answers you give to all questions.

13. *Do be prepared to take an oath.*
    In adversary proceedings such as arbitration, the
    swearing of witnesses is often preferred, whether
    required by statute or not (it is not required
    under the common law). If either party requests
    the swearing of witnesses, the arbitrator will ordi-
    narily oblige them. In swearing witnesses, the arbi-
    trator asks the witness if he solemnly swears that

the testimony he is about to give in the case is the truth, the whole truth, and nothing but the truth, so help him God. The witness, with right hand raised, answers, "I do."

14. *Don't repeat questions before answering them.*
This gives the appearance of stalling to buy time to conjure up an answer that will best serve your interests. The truth should be stated with more spontaneity.

15. *Don't stall, or delay, or fuss and fidget.*
Try to answer questions with reasonable promptness, without squirming or fidgeting. Such behavior merely casts suspicion on your credibility.

16. *Do be neatly groomed.*
It is not necessary to be in a suit and tie, nor dressed up in any way. It is merely desirable that you appear as clean and as neatly groomed as you can under the circumstances.

17. *Don't mumble.*
Speak clearly. Your testimony is of value only if it is understood by the arbiter. He may interpret unclear utterances as a form of evasiveness.

18. *Do not answer a question if your advocate raises an objection.*
If your advocate raises an objection (probably during cross-examination), take a deep breath and relax. Don't continue testifying until the arbitrator tells you to. The reasons for your advocate's objection may not always be very clear to you, but you can be sure it is intended to be in your best interests.

19. *Do keep your hands away from your face.*
Preferably hold your hands still or fold them comfortably on your lap. Covering your mouth conveys an impression of nervousness, tension, uncertainty, or evasiveness, all of which reflect poorly on your credibility.

20. *Do advise your advocate of all pocket memos, diaries, notes, etc.*

If you have any notes you previously made at the time the grievance occurred which are relevant to the case, review them with your advocate when he is preparing the case for trial. He may or may not elect to use them, but don't surprise him with them at the hearing. Under certain circumstances they may be useful as supportive or corroborative of your oral testimony.

21. *Do quietly advise your advocate if you hear testimony which reminds you of a relevant matter*
No one has a perfect memory. You may unintentionally overlook some point you know about the case. If something at the hearing provokes your recall of a previously overlooked and relevant matter, pass a note to your advocate.

22. *Do suggest a recess to your advocate if you think it would be beneficial.*
Listen carefully and watch attentively. If you hear or see something occur which you fear has not been noticed by your advocate, pass a note or whisper to him suggesting a recess. But he must decide whether to call for one, for he is the strategist, tactician, and quarterback for your side.

23. *Don't deny you are being paid while testifying.*
If you are on salary, you probably will be being paid while testifying. Readily admit it. You are not being paid to induce you to give certain favorable testimony, though that is what such a question tries to infer. Be truthful. Don't worry about honest admissions. Your advocate will clarify the point with the arbitrator if any confusion follows your honest admission of being paid and why.

24. *Don't look to your advocate for answers to questions.*
The answers to questions asked of you must come from you. If the arbiter sees you getting signs or nods or head shakes from someone else, he may discredit all or most of your testimony.

25. *Don't contradict yourself.*
A witness who contradicts himself always leaves

the arbitrator with some doubt about his testimony, at least with respect to those questions he answers contradictorily, and perhaps with a residue of doubt about the rest. If the other side testified certainly on the same points on which you have been inconsistent or contradictory, the arbitrator may well resolve his doubt in favor of the other party.

26. *Do realize cross-examination is not limited to the subjects of direct examination.*
Since the arbitrator has a paramount interest in securing all of the facts, he may refuse to restrict cross-examination to matters brought out in direct examination, and he can be expected not to limit the number of re-cross or re-direct examinations. But while the parties are allowed considerable latitude in cross-examining witnesses to reveal conflicts in their testimony and to challenge credibility, arbitrators will not condone personal invective against witnesses.

27. *Don't contact the arbitrator outside the hearing.*
Before a hearing has been held and after it has been closed, the arbitrator should be contacted only by the principals who handled the case for the parties. Witnesses should not be in contact with the arbitrator.

28. *Don't bring prepared lists of questions into the hearing room.*
The company advocate may prepare a list of questions he intends to ask you, or which he anticipates you may be asked on cross-examination, to help you familiarize yourself with the questions and the procedure. Don't bring these questions with you into the hearing room.

29. *Do realize witnesses may be excluded from the hearing room when not testifying.*
One of the traditional methods for preserving the purity of testimony is the rule that witnesses may be excluded from the hearing chamber during the testimony of others. Whenever either party invokes

it, it is invariably granted. This is to guard against the possibility that one witness may be influenced by what he has heard someone else say. It also highlights the importance of each witness telling the truth, so each account coincides with others.

30. *Do understand that an interested party has a right to be present.*
    Direct or interested parties, for example, the grievant or aggrieved individuals, do have the right to remain in the hearing room during all testimony from all witnesses.

31. *Do bring a note-pad and pencil to the hearing with you.*
    You may help your advocate by being alert and attentive to all that transpires during the hearing. You are free to quietly pass notes to him so long as you don't interfere with the proceedings.

32. *Do speak plainly and clearly.*
    The information you bring forth is only helpful to your case if it is clearly understood by the arbitrator. This won't happen unless your words are audible.

33. *Don't you as a witness raise any objections.*
    A witness who himself objects to questions and tries to avoid answering them will create an impression that he is unwilling to make full and frank disclosure. A very few matters are matters of personal privilege, which must be asserted by the witness, but if they are likely to arise, the witness and the advocate should have a common understanding of the procedure for asserting the privilege.

34. *Do understand that the grievant need not testify.*
    An employee may refuse to testify in arbitration by the exercise of a privilege against self-incrimination, but he does so at his own risk. Because the grievant is often able to cast light upon the dispute, he ordinarily does take the witness stand. Failure of a grievant to testify at the hearing of his grievance has in some cases been a factor in the arbitrator's conclusion that the grievance lacked

merit. However, arbitrators sometimes have expressly stated that the failure of a grievant to testify creates no inference against him; yet an arbitrator may pointedly note that the grievant's failure to testify has left the case against him unre-
futed, where the company has adequately established its case by probative evidence.

35. *Do study carefully any contract provisions appli-
    cable to the case.*
    You are not expected to be an expert on the
    contract. But you should have at least a working
    knowledge of the relevant provisions if you were
    interpreting or applying them in connection with
    some decisions you made, or action you took.

36. *Don't interrupt the hearing while you're not tes-
    tifying.*
    This type of conduct reflects negatively on you
    and on your side. An arbitrator is only human.
    Don't engage in conduct which will prejudice him
    in any way against you or your side.

37. *Do realize the arbitrator may also ask you ques-
    tions.*
    The arbiter is privileged to ask questions of wit-
    nesses to clarify a point, or to obtain information
    additional to that proffered, or even to inquire into
    new areas. Just as in direct and cross-examination,
    be courteous, honest, and forthright in the answers
    you provide.

38. *Do realize the cross-examiner may use harsh or
    aggressive tactics.*
    The objectives of cross-examination may be classi-
    fied into four groups: (1) discrediting the testi-
    mony of the witness; (2) using the testimony of
    this witness to discredit the unfavorable testimony
    of other witnesses; (3) using the testimony of this
    witness to corroborate the favorable testimony of
    other witnesses; and (4) using the testimony of
    this witness to contribute independently to the
    favorable development of one's own case. Different
    tactics are used to accomplish different aims. It is

not uncommon for the cross-examiner to use an aggressive manner or even harsh tactics. But do not let this get to you or upset you. Be calm, cool, and self-assured. The arbitrator is carefully evaluating you, your behavior, and your remarks.

39. *Do realize that questions, ones worded to suggest a desired answer, are permissible during cross-examination.*

A question is leading if it suggests to the witness the answer the interrogator desires. Listen carefully and give a considered, intelligent, and honest response, even though it may (as it most often is) be different than the suggested and obviously desired answer. Don't be drawn into an answer which you don't basically agree with, in an effort to be agreeable with the questioner.

40. *Do control yourself.*

It is the legitimate role of the cross-examiner to try to upset you, make you lose your temper, cause you to make intemperate, contradictory, or confused remarks. Once again, you are not responsible for his behavior, only for your own. Be calm, cool, self-assured, and in control of your actions and words. The arbitrator will be evaluating you, your answers, and your demeanor. You want him to leave the hearing with a positive impression of you and your credibility.

41. *Do realize the cross-examiner may shift the subject of inquiry suddenly and frequently.*

The theory of the "hop, skip, and jump" method of cross-examination is that the witness is kept so busy shifting his thought processes from one subject to another that he will not have time to formulate answers to fit some dishonest scheme, or that if he does so his answers will be so artless that the advocate will be able to expose them. You needn't worry about such questioning if all of your responses are thoughtfully considered and honest in context.

Ordinarily a witness should testify as to facts. If he branches out into what is merely his opinion, he is invading the province of the arbitrator. However, experts, persons with special training or skill in a particular field, may testify not only as to facts but also to their opinions on matters pertaining to their field. Their special qualifications and knowledge are presumed to make their opinions trustworthy and enlightened. A company official, a highly skilled tradesman, an engineer, a medical man may have such special skills, training, and experience as to qualify them to state opinions on technical matters or to demonstrate a method of procedure.

Witnesses should be used only if they are essential for the production of certain information which is not otherwise available through records, documents, or files. They are potentially the weakest link in a case. Witnesses are invariably exposed to cross-examination. There's no such thing as a perfect witness – though a witness often leaves the stand unscathed and with his party's case not injured by his testimony. But the reverse potential is always present – and too often such potential is realized. Witnesses should only be used where there is no other way to bring out the information they possess.

7
Arbitration and Advocacy

The Advocate

Two experienced labor relations practitioners may meet identical situations with wholly different methods and each achieve success. One may be dramatic and witty, while another uses low-key methods to emphasize the earnestness of the appeal. Each has developed a distinctive talent for presenting a cause persuasively. Undoubtedly those who become the most effective advocates begin with native ability to think accurately under pressure and to speak extemporaneously, but this is only a beginning. Other practitioners with less native ability may prove more effective because they prepare more thoroughly and apply methods best suited to their own peculiar talents and limitations.

Very few persons can effectively assume numerous roles. Attempts to assume a demeanor that is unnatural usually only suggest to the arbitrator that something is being put over on him. Whatever method you consider, be sure there is no serious danger that it will imply a lack of sincerity. Use only those roles you can actually live with.

Probably you will be at your best as an advocate when you cause the arbitrator to believe that the decision you are urging upon him is the decision you would reach yourself.

The beneficial effect of your sincerity may be greatly reduced, perhaps to nothing, if you seem willing to use any means available, fair or unfair, to advance your cause. Granted, an advocate is often more intent upon winning than upon getting a fair hearing—though to the advocate the two may be synonymous. An advocate's bias is usually excused, though not ignored; but the advocate's methods may be viewed more critically. If you clearly ask only a fair hearing—no less and no more—an arbitrator will generally respond sympathetically. This is particularly true if there is an apparent contrast between the opposing advocates: the one who resorts to methods that seem unfair, or to contentions that seem technical or tricky, incurs disfavor.

Long range, beyond your concern with the immediate case, you have an interest in avoiding habitual use of methods designed to win cases on technical grounds only. A reputation for this type of practice becomes a handicap in future cases.

To be an effective advocate you must maintain perspective. Consider each problem in its proper relationship to the development of the case as a whole. Let your decision to make a certain point—to ask a certain question, to raise a certain objection, or to use a certain technique—be guided not solely by its technical soundness and immediate hope of advantage, but also by the effect of a point upon the arbitrator's consideration of the case as a whole. Likewise, let your timing for raising the point be guided by the effect of timing upon the reactions of the arbitrator.

Last but not least, there is no substitute for thorough preparation. This means preparation of (1) contract, (2) facts, and (3) argument. It means not only knowing the presentation of your own side of the case but also knowing the other side well enough to anticipate your adversary's evidence and case theories. It means discovering the weak points as well as the strong points of the case. In short, know the whole case.

The Case

Opening the Case

An opening statement is intended to acquaint the arbitrator with the essential facts of the case. It should primarily be an outline of the cause of action or the defense, but a skillful opening will be more than that. It will also create a favorable atmosphere for the reception of the evidence to be offered and for the position taken by the party.

An opening statement should be brief, clear, and direct. It should tell the story in logical sequence—chronological order is usually easiest for the arbitrator to follow. There should be no argument and no peroration, but in the development of the story the important facts should be emphasized. Address yourself to your own proof; do not tell the arbitrator what the other side cannot prove.

There should be no overstatement. It is dangerous to mention anything which you are not positive you will be able to prove. Promise less rather than more. Reserve the strong statement for your summation. And reserve some of the details of the evidence for development on the witness stand, so that the arbitrator's interest may be sustained. That does not mean, however, that any essential fact should be kept in the background.

The opening statement should be planned, not improvised. Having prepared his own opening in advance of the hearing, the advocate is free to listen attentively—as he should—to his adversary's opening so that he may know what to expect in the way of proof by the other side.

Know your case so thoroughly that you can tell it with flowing continuity, without notes or stammering pauses or coattail-pulling by an associate. No matter how long or how complicated your case may be, it is your duty to know every detail backward and forward. If you do not, you will start off the whole hearing on the wrong foot.

You cannot inspire confidence and engender faith where you have none yourself, and you can have none if you have not planned thoroughly. This is such a fundamental principle, not only for opening statements, but for the whole case, that it should be engraved on every trial advocate's mind.

You may have heard of trial lawyers who boast that they require no preparation and can pick up the case as it goes along. Do not admire or emulate them. All the best known trial lawyers of this country achieved success in court largely by hard work before they ever took their cases to court, and when they got there they knew every fact in detail. The outstanding trial attorney boasts not of how little but of how hard he has worked in the preparation of his case. The outstanding arbitral advocate does the same.

The thorough knowledge of every fact in your case will give you the calm and the poise which are so important in the hearing room. Your mind will be completely at ease because you are free from haunting uncertainty and doubt. You cannot have poise, confidence, and an active presence of mind when you are beset by inward misgivings.

But it is not enough to know your case thoroughly. You must also present it in simple, understandable fashion. An advocate may know his case thoroughly but lack the ability to explain it so another can understand. As in the telling of any story, there must be a definite continuity. In every case, without exception, the arbitrator must be fully acquainted with what the issues are, i.e., with what is involved and what questions he must decide. Keep to the chronological sequence of events as much as possible. In cases where there are many separate events, spaced at varying intervals, and where dates are important, it is almost imperative that a chronology be followed. By this method the various events will stand in proper relationship to each other.

Effective presentation obviously involves a consideration of how the case as a whole should be handled.

There is a general awareness of the favorable reaction which understatement produces. It carries within itself an implication of fairness and strength; it engenders a feeling of confidence which exaggeration destroys. Like others, arbitrators draw the most favorable inferences from a framework of understatement.

A good case may be lost because of exaggerations which an opposing advocate can demolish by testimony or cross-examination.

Similarly, exaggerated claims that cannot be supported by testimony result in an apparent failure of proof which the opposing advocate may build upon. Moreover, understatement of claims provides a better background for the testimony of witnesses because the proof then seems even stronger by contrast.

Direct Examination

The immediate aims of direct examination are: (1) to present evidence sufficient to raise each claim or defense—to complete a record of testimony that will support your arguments; and (2) to convince the factfinder, the arbitrator, of the truthfulness and accuracy of all the evidence supporting your claim or defense.

Although effective direct examination is usually less spectacular, more cases are won on direct than on cross-examination. In the ordinary hearing, the original development of all elements of a claim depends almost entirely upon direct examination. As the advocate, you may plan to use cross-examination of opposing witnesses to support the case you developed on direct examination to persuade the arbitrator. But do not rely on cross-examination of your adversary's witnesses to supply any element that you can supply by direct examination.

You may appropriately place greater reliance on cross-examination in planning a defense than in planning the development of your own case. The defense is often a denial, rather than an affirmative assertion. When you are dealing with a nondiscipline case, one involving contract interpretation, your problem is to convince the arbitrator that vital elements of the opponent's case are not supported in fact, or to convince the arbitrator that the other party has failed to prove some vital element of fact. Also, you can cross-examine the opposition's witnesses before you call your own; if your plans for cross-examination go awry, you have an opportunity to recover. For an affirmative defense, it is better in precase planning not to rely upon cross-examination; at least prepare an alternative plan for developing each element by your own witnesses in case cross-examination does not go according to plan.

Using Cumulative Witnesses

Using corroborative testimony or cumulative witnesses is a purely tactical decision. Calling cumulative witnesses is a highly dangerous practice. If they testify alike, their testimony is suspect because people do not observe and remember events in exactly the same way. If they differ, the argument is that the witnesses are poor observers, or otherwise unreliable. Of course, you may vouch for the honesty of your witnesses and your case, but you never know whether the arbitrator will be convinced. More important, however, is the danger of contradictions on important matters, especially when the cross-examination is skillful.

The Order of Witnesses

Your decision on the order of witnesses may be influenced by such practical factors as the availability of particular witnesses whose convenience you must serve to secure their cooperation. Such factors can be a detriment to the most effective presentation of the case; but through careful planning you can usually eliminate their influence and almost always reduce it.

Logical progression in the story of the case, developed through testimony, is an asset. It helps the arbitrator to understand and remember the testimony.

The first and last witnesses are particularly important. Most observers agree that first impressions tend to last; once the arbitrator has formed an impression, the burden is on the one who seeks to change it. Therefore, present a strong and favorable witness as the first witness in the case.

The last witness occupies a special position because the memory of what he says is freshest in the mind of the arbitrator during his formal deliberation. It is especially helpful if that freshest memory is the memory of a strong and favorable witness. Accordingly, use a strong witness first and a strong witness last, and let other factors govern the order of the witnesses in between.

The special importance of the first and last witnesses is but one aspect of a broader proposition that the timing of evidence may materially affect is effect upon the arbitrator.

Through careful planning, unfavorable evidence can be offered at a time calculated to reduce the notice it receives, and favorable evidence can be offered at a time that will give it greater emphasis.

Sometimes the testimony of one witness is necessary to lay a foundation for the testimony of another. Your failure to consider this factor may result in delay, the necessity for recalling witnesses, and even failure to secure admission of material evidence because you were unable to get an essential witness to return to provide a predicate.

The need for logical presentation of the theory of your case may be served by effective use of the right to make an oral statement of the claim before any evidence is offered. Also, in selecting witnesses for appearance on the stand, you may give a weaker witness the opportunity of observing the other witnesses in the proceedings. He may thereby become more at ease when he takes the stand so that he can state his case more effectively. The danger of damaging mistakes in a witness's testimony is reduced when he has the opportunity to hear the testimony of his supporting witnesses and to observe the techniques of the opposing advocate on cross-examination before he takes the stand.

Preparing an Outline of Testimony

A spontaneous statement is the most convincing statement. If you could know that spontaneous, unplanned direct examination would produce only favorable statements, you could avoid anything even suggesting a plan or outline for fear of interfering with that convincing spontaneity. Unfortunately that condition can never exist. Direct examination without planning is, therefore, a gamble. It may still be a gamble after the most thorough planning, but at least the odds are more favorable. Rarely, there is a combination of witness and advocate capable of effective direct examination without advance preparation, but preparation is necessary for most advocates and helpful to all. The goal is planning that causes the least possible interference with the spontaneity of the testimony, consistent with reasonable assurance that it will not develop unfavorably. A conflict exists here between the interest in encouraging a convincing way of testifying and the interest in assuring that the substance of the testimony is favorable. The degree to which one interest is favored over the other in any single case must be a matter of judgment in the light of the circumstances.

Interview of the witness while the facts are fresh in his mind, written or recorded statements, the analysis of contract wording and past practice to determine what facts must be proved to support a cause of action, the comparison of the witness's statement with physical facts and other expected testimony—all of these, as well as the final witness interviews, are, in a sense, merely steps in the planning of the direct examination of the witness.

An arbitrator is no doubt favorably impressed by spontaneity of answers of the witnesses. But he does not expect spontaneity in interrogation. Any good labor relations practitioner plans his work. Accordingly, it is no disadvantage that the course of interrogation reveals to an arbitrator that it has been carefully planned.

The advantages of outlining the examination of each witness are many. Your presentation is more logical and orderly, less confused and wasteful of time; you can check your outline of the examination of all witnesses against your outline of the essential fact elements of your case; you are less likely to omit some vital evidence in the stress of the hearing; and you can more easily anticipate and provide against objections to your important evidence. You will usually find it worthwhile to make a detailed outline of the proposed cross-examination as well as direct examination of every known witness. The more experience you gain, the more of this outlining you can do mentally, without reducing it to writing.

Another advantage of outlining the examination of each witness in advance is that it enables you to open and close the testimony of the witness on the stronger points and in other ways to arrange the timing of evidence for the greatest tactical benefit.

But whether the outline is written or mental, it is not final. It is merely a tool to be used in the hearing, and should not be slavishly followed. Actual developments in the hearing will demand variations from it.

Framing Questions

By anticipating accurately the subject matter you will cover with each witness, you can frame your questions in advance, testing each question to see whether it is leading or not. In due course, that practice will help you develop good habits of framing questions, so that your phrasing of even extemporaneous questions will meet the requirements of proper interrogation. The following suggestions are intended for advance preparation of specific questions and for use in developing good habits in the phrasing of questions:

1. Ask only one question at a time. Compound sentences are sometimes hard to understand. Answers to compound questions are worse; they are likely to be incomplete, ambiguous, or otherwise misleading.

2. Avoid negatives. Consider: Q – "You do not know whether Jones was there?" A – "Yes." Did the witness mean "Yes, I know" or did he mean "Yes, it is true that I do not know," or did he mean "Yes, Jones was there." If you notice it, this doubt can be cleared by another question and the loss is simply delay and a slight danger of confusion. But if you failed to clarify an exchange such as this, you risk having the answer interpreted differently from what you know the witness meant.

3. Make the question brief. Both the witness and the arbitrator must understand the whole question in order to understand it correctly.

4. State the question in simple words. You want the arbitrator to understand both the questions and the answers, and this requires words used in everyday conversation. This is not a recommendation for use of slang or bad grammar, however; that practice, unless it comes naturally to the

advocate, probably will be resented as talking down to the arbitrator.

5. In summary, make the question clear. It is not enough that you and the witness understand each other's questions and answers—though of course that is important. The arbitrator is the one whose understanding is your primary interest. He is less familiar with the facts and the circumstances than either you or the witness. It is no reflection on the intelligence of arbitrators that simple questions are best.

Leading the Witness

A question is leading if it suggests to the witness the answer that the interrogator desires. The vice of the question is telling the witness what the advocate wants him to say. Having received the message, the witness can then answer a nonleading question in the desired way, even though the leading question is stricken. Consequently, you may sometimes be tempted to ask a leading question deliberately, realizing that an objection to it will be sustained, but using it to coach the witness.

However, some types of leading questions are permitted:

(1) Questions as to preliminary matters which set the stage for inquiries relevant to the material issues in the case;

(2) Questions that the witness has already answered;

(3) Questions addressed to an adverse or hostile witness;

(4) Questions on cross-examination of a witness called by the adversary.

Leading questions may also be allowed (a) to a witness of limited understanding, (b) to a witness whose recollection has been exhausted but who is supposed to know additional facts material to the case, and (c) to a witness who is being asked to contradict statements previously made by other witnesses.

Pursuing inquiries by leading the witnesses may cast a cloud of suspicion not only upon that particular statement but also upon other testimony of the witness and even upon still other evidence you later offer. Whether you should take that risk will depend upon how important the evidence is to the case.

The use of leading questions has tactical disadvantages. The practice may result in repeated rulings of the arbitrator sustaining objections—and perhaps reprimanding the advocate. Although labor relations practitioners in arbitration generally prefer to avoid objections for fear of impressing the arbitrator unfavorably, most consider that objections of this type, sustained by the arbitrator, are more damaging to the interrogator than to the objector.

Certainly arbitrators frown on the practice of leading witnesses. Furthermore, even if no objections are made, it is dangerous to assume that the interrogation is developing favorably. The rule against leading questions is no more than a rule of common sense: if you want the witness's own story, you must depend upon the witness's statement of it, not on the advocate's. This is the common sense rule that arbitrators are likely to apply. And, of course, your adversary may frame objections so as to help the arbitrator reach that conclusion.

Expert Witnesses

When using expert witnesses, you should prove their qualifications. This serves two purposes: (1) it lays the foundation for admissibility of opinion testimony, and (2) it persuades the arbitrator that the findings and opinions of the expert are accurate. Your adversary may suggest a waiver of the proof of qualification—particularly if the expert's qualifications are outstanding—in an attempt to prevent the arbitrator from hearing an impressive array of credentials. You are not necessarily bound to accept such a waiver; if the qualifications are impressive, you should proceed nonetheless to prove them. On the other hand, laboring over insignificant details of background and experience will merely bore the arbitrator and perhaps give him the impression you are trying to build up the witness beyond what the facts justify. There is also a possible advantage in omitting some details so the witness may have something further to offer should your adversary choose to cross-examine him regarding his qualifications. Also try to keep the arbitrator from inferring that the expert is a professional witness whose testimony can be bought, or that he is biased in favor of one group.

An expert witness is particularly valuable because he may testify as to opinion, while other witnesses are limited to facts—what they saw, heard, experienced through their various senses.

Demonstrative Evidence

The traditional way of proving a fact is by asking a witness who knows, and some hearings include only that type of evidence. Yet this type of evidence is in most respects the least convincing type you can offer. It is subject to all the frailties of human errors of observation, memory, expression, and integrity. It is common knowledge that two witnesses standing side by side observing the same event will, if interrogated separately, differ about what occurred. Arbitrators who are not already aware of this can usually be persuaded by moderate attention in the advocate's argument. The advocate who has more real, or demonstrative, evidence than his adversary has a distinct advantage. Chances for error are reduced or absent in the case of demonstrative evidence.

Generally, you should make use of all the favorable physical or demonstrative evidence available to you. Careful attention and some imagination will disclose that more is available than is customarily used in the trial of cases.

Although any diagram made by the witness is no better than his observation, memory, and ability to draw, a diagram by one with average ability and drawing can be superior to a simple description; it may convey to the arbitrator more accurately than mere statement the idea that is in the witness's mind. A diagram or other type of drawing has another distinct value: it preserves the expression of the idea, so that the arbitrator may turn back to it to refresh his own memory of the testimony.

However, you should never ask a witness on direct examination to prepare a drawing or a diagram unless you have previously determined that the witness can do it reasonably well. Some witnesses are so poor at drawing, particularly at keeping a reasonably accurate scale and relative position of various objects, that more harm than good will be done by asking that a drawing be made in the presence of the arbitrator.

If you plan to use a map prepared by another during the testimony of a witness, show the map to the witness in the prehearing conference. Take care, however, in discussing the map with your witness, to prepare for the possibility that he will be asked on cross-examination if you showed him where he should place certain marks on the map. He should not deny that you have properly asked him to advise you where he will place the marks if asked to do so; denial would be almost as damaging as proof that you actually told the witness where to place the marks.

When using a drawing, should you ask that it be on a blackboard or on paper? Should you ask the witness to start from a blank or should you furnish a skilled drawing of background objects already authenticated by previous evidence? An advantage of drawing on paper is that you can offer it in evidence when it is completed; and the arbitrator who is permitted to take exhibits with him then may carry it with him for his ultimate deliberations. Whether to start from a blank or not will depend on your witness's drawing skill.

Cross-Examination
The Art of Cross-Examination
To excel in cross-examination you must have some native ability, but if you are interested in arbitration work, you probably have this kind of ability to some degree in any case. You can develop your native cross-examination ability, like musical ability, by practice and experience. But the

talent for cross-examination, though necessary, is the lesser part of effective cross-examination. Nearly all effective cross-examination is to some degree planned. Through adequate planning you can often cross-examine effectively even before you have any substantial experience. As you gain experience, your success in cross-examination will continue to depend on your diligence in preparing.

The potential aims of cross-examination are four: (1) discrediting the testimony of the witness; (2) using the testimony of this witness to discredit the unfavorable testimony of other witnesses; (3) using the testimony of this witness to corroborate the favorable testimony of other witnesses; and (4) using the testimony of this witness to contribute independently to the favorable development of your own case.

A method of cross-examination designed to serve one aim may defeat another. Adequate planning requires an appraisal of the relative advantages associated with each of these aims, since this is a factor bearing on the choice of methods.

Your selection of methods of cross-examination will depend also on the type of witness you face; among other things, the age, education, and mentality of the witness are important. The most ignorant witness is often the hardest to cross-examine because you cannot manage him as well. Also, you must exercise great care to avoid creating sympathy for him because you are exposing his ignorance or illiteracy. You must condemn testimony as unreliable without condemning the witness as ignorant. If you ridicule an ignorant witness, or treat him sarcastically, the arbitrator may think you are taking an unfair advantage of the difference in intelligence and education between yourself and the witness.

Usually it is best to adopt an attitude of courtesy toward the witness, for although the arbitrator expects you to be an advocate, he may very quickly develop sympathy for a witness whom he thinks you are badgering. It is quite possible to be very polite and yet convey to the arbitrator your distrust of the witness's testimony.

Aids to Cross-Examination

Your preparation for cross-examination begins when you first investigate the case. Maximum success in cross-examination depends on the kind of investigation that lets you know your adversary's case and evidence as well as your own. And knowing what the witnesses probably will say is important for deciding not only what to ask but what not to ask.

With thorough investigation you can realize instantly, during your adversary's direct examination, the implications of the questions and the answers. Investigation also provides tools for cross-examination, including written statements, documents and records, and information concerning actions and statements of the witness to which other persons will testify. Taking into consideration the aims of your cross-examination, the aids available, and the subjects of inquiry, prepare an outline of the proposed cross-examination of each witness you expect your adversary to use. You can expect to vary from the outline more than in direct examination of your own witness, but the previous consideration of expected problems will still be most helpful.

The Decision to Cross-Examine

Should you cross-examine each witness? Most stories about cross-examination tell of the brilliant questioning that won the law suit. Others tell of the inept cross-examination that lost it. Both types, though influenced by a kind of "poetic license," are founded on truths.

The risks of cross-examination include the following:

1. Confronting a witness with a prior written statement inconsistent with his present testimony may result in proof of other facts recorded in the statement;

2. Confronting the witness with inconsistencies between his testimony and that of your own witness may result in impeachment of your own witness;

3. An attempt to prove or even actual proof of bad character of the witness may provoke the sympathy of the arbitrator not only for the witness but also for the case he supports;

4. Cross-examination to reveal indirectly the bias of the witness by committing him to an extreme may merely strengthen the direct examination;

5. Cross-examination intended to bring out matters about which your adversary failed to inquire, in the belief that the answers will be favorable to your client, may result only in more evidence favorable to the adverse party;

6. Calling on the witness to repeat and elaborate his testimony, as a foundation for proof of prior contradictions or inconsistencies, may emphasize and strengthen the witness's testimony, especially if his explanation of the apparent inconsistencies is plausible;

7. Cross-examination intended to show animosity associated with termination of employment may provoke sympathy for the discharged employee;

8. Asking a "why" question in the belief that the witness can have no reasonable explanation may result in his making prejudicial arguments that would have been clearly inadmissible otherwise;

9. Insistence upon a clear answer from an evasive witness may lead to an unexpected and unfavorable disclosure;

10. Cross-examination of an expert concerning his qualifications may simply bolster the proof of those qualifications;

11. Cross-examination intended to exact disclosures from an unwilling witness may cause the arbitrator to consider your methods unfair.

For each risk there is a corresponding possibility of gain. And you incur the risks no matter how carefully your cross-examination is planned to achieve gains. Proceeding without an aim and a plan would involve the risks without any corresponding hope of benefit.

Planning is essential to the most effective cross-examination. The plan for cross-examination should not be inflexible; nor should the cross-examination be haphazard. Even those who change the subject of inquiry frequently and suddenly in cross-examination do so with a purpose; they hope that the truth will out because the witness does not have time to anticipate the next question and fabricate an answer, or that quickly conceived untruths will be so artless that they can be exposed.

Careful planning may reduce but will never wholly eliminate the risk of harm from cross-examination. The decision to cross-examine a particular witness, and to what extent and with what aims and methods, calls for accepting a calculated risk. This weighing of risks is something that as an arbitration advocate you must do frequently, not only with respect to cross-examination but even to such broader questions as whether to proceed to arbitration or to settle.

That cases are sometimes lost in cross-examination is reason enough to beware of an unyielding rule that you cross-examine every witness. Yet failure to cross-examine a witness may lead the arbitrator to conclude that you concede the truth of his testimony, or that you have nothing with which to dispute it. In rare instances the testimony of your adversary's witness is so favorable or so sound and undisputed that you are willing to adopt it, and you may even smile warmly as you say, "We have no questions." When you are not willing to adopt the witness's testimony, it probably is sound not to release a witness without some cross-examination unless the inference of acquiescence can be met successfully with an argument that either is apparent or probably will be accepted by the arbitrator when it is pointed out to him.

Assuming that you have decided to cross-examine, you are faced with the problem as to length and content of the cross-examination. Most of the questions discussed here are relevant, though of course not all of them can be presented in a single situation. Also, the possibility of recross-examination, in case your adversary uses redirect, must be considered; the tactical implications are substantially identical with those involved in determining when and how to use redirect examination.

Using Inconsistent Statements

Should you confront a witness on cross-examination with inconsistencies between his testimony and his prior oral and written statements? When and how should you use a written statement for impeachment?

By confronting a witness with inconsistencies you can (1) emphasize the contradiction in the mind of the arbitrator by bringing together contradictory evidence that appeared at different times during the course of the hearing (impeachment of a witness in this way also casts doubt on the value of his testimony on other subjects as well as the subject of the contradiction); and (2) upset the witness and thus improve your chances of obtaining admissions on other subjects.

These ends are best served by confronting the witness with his own contradictions—inconsistencies between answers on direct examination and on cross-examination, or between testimony at the hearing and prior statements (sworn or unsworn, oral or written), or between his testimony and his pleading or demand or formal claim. You may sometimes serve the same ends, however, by confronting the witness with inconsistencies between his testimony and that of other witnesses.

Against the potential of beneficial results from using inconsistencies, and from your timing of your use, you must weigh the risks. Consider the problem of inconsistency between testimony at the hearing and a prior written statement. The first question is whether to use the statement at all. The statement may contain other matter that is favorable to the party who called the witness and has as yet not been proved; using the statement would probably result in proof of that matter by independent questions of opposing counsel even if that part of the statement itself were not received in evidence over an objection. If the overall effect of the statement is less favorable to your client than the overall effect of the witness's testimony, don't use the statement. Unless the contradictions are on important matters, the value of proving them is outweighed by the harm to your case in other respects.

If you decide to use the statement, how do you proceed? (Indeed, after considering various ways, you may decide not to use it after all.) Two distinct methods of use are possible: (1) using the statement in the cross-examination itself; and (2) introducing the statement separately after the witness has left the stand. Because it is rarely advisable or effective to authenticate a written statement by a person other than the one who wrote it, the decision will probably be to use the statement on cross-examination or not at all. Moreover, the arbitrator might well wonder why the witness himself had not been asked about his own statement and given an opportunity to explain. Finally, since it is a case of self-contradiction by the witness, the effect is much more dramatic if you confront the witness directly. So you should generally use the statement on cross-examination rather than solely by introducing it separately. If the witness repudiates the statement on cross-examination, however, either as a whole or by contending that he did not read it over and that it contains errors, consider authenticating the statement by testimony of a witness to the statement or of the person who took it.

If you are using the statement on cross-examination, how will you lay the foundation for it? Should you produce the statement and ask the witness to identify it first, as a predicate for the questions about the statement and its contents? Or should you postpone production of the statement until you have asked questions about the subject matter and about the circumstances of taking the statement?

The practice of holding a statement in view though not referring to it verbally is sometimes used when the advocate wants to frighten the witness but does not want to introduce the statement itself because of some risk of harm. Even this use of a statement that you do not want in evidence involves a risk, however. Your opponent may call upon you to produce the statement; if you withhold it or object to its being placed in evidence by your opponent, the arbitrator may draw unfavorable inferences. It is possible that you could evade the problem by refusing to show the statement

to your adversary without an agreement in advance that it
can be received in evidence—of course, with the expectation that your adversary will not agree. But that attitude is
likely to cause unfavorable reaction to your unfair methods;
your adversary will not seem unreasonable in refusing to
agree to reception of a statement he has never seen.

Usually the use of a contradictory statement in cross-
examination is more effective if you can get the witness
thoroughly committed on all material points before you
produce the statement. There is also a greater likelihood
that you will catch the witness so completely off guard that
the arbitrator can see it. He has less time to steel himself for
the blow than when you have been looking at the statement
while asking questions.

Should you confront a witness on cross-examination
with inconsistencies between his testimony and that of
others? Here, you must consider the relative advantages and
disadvantages as compared with other possible uses of the
same materials. The best answer will depend to some extent
on the identity and relationship of the witnesses, the nature
of the inconsistency, and its significance to the case. If the
inconsistency is between the testimony of two witnesses,
both called by your opponent, confronting either witness
with the inconsistencies should at least emphasize in the
mind of the arbitrator the fact of contradiction. The degree
of benefit will depend upon how serious the contradiction
is, but usually there is no better way to make the most of it.

Rarely will much be gained by confronting a party with
an inconsistency between his testimony and that of his
adversary. His answer is obvious: the adversary is wrong. It
may be desirable, however, to point out the inconsistency,
without forcing the issue, so that the witness has an opportunity to call his adversary a liar. If he is the type who might
do that, he is likely to do at least some damage to his own
cause.

There is a further edge to this type of inconsistency. It
may reflect unfavorably on the testimony of your own
witness if the witness you are cross-examining offers satis-

factory support for his own version. Before pressing the witness about such an inconsistency, therefore, be prepared to corroborate the version of your own witness, or to introduce other evidence tending to impeach your adversary's witness. If you have neither of these and the inconsistency is not crucial to your case, ignore the inconsistency as long as your adversary is content to do so.

The nature of the inconsistency and its significance have an important bearing on whether you should point it up, and when. If you try to make much of obviously trivial matters, you will at best amuse the arbitrator and at worst cause him to think you are trying to confuse the issues rather than seeking a fair and sound disposition. But the problem is primarily one of timing. If the inconsistency is one of observation, memory, or expression, the best way to use it is usually to confront the witness with it on cross-examination. On the other hand, if the inconsistency reflects on the integrity of your opposing party or a key witness, you may make more dramatic and effective use of it by preparing the background during cross-examination and introducing the actual inconsistency later with your convincing, independent evidence of the falsity of the testimony.

Inquiring into Source of Knowledge

Careful inquiry will often disclose that things the witness says as if they were his own observations are actually only repetition of what some other person has told him. If you ask a person unfamiliar with rules of evidence whether he can state a fact "of his own knowledge," he may think the correct answer is "yes" if he has been informed of the fact by someone whom he considers reliable. Although arbitrators have not adopted a philosopher's definition of "knowing," their definition *is* more restrictive than the ordinary layman's understanding; the witness is not able to speak of his own knowledge if he is merely repeating what he has been told, regardless of the reliability of the informant. His testimony that someone else made the statement, when offered to prove the truth of the matter stated, is excluded by the hearsay rule unless some exception applies. His repetition as

his own statement of the matter he heard is excluded because he himself did not personally perceive what happened.
A showing of personal knowledge of certain facts may also be
essential as a predicate for the admission of opinion evidence.
A witness might therefore be asked how he knows the facts
he is testifying about.

Inquiring into New Subjects

Occasionally a witness called by your adversary will be the
only possible source of particular evidence favorable to
your case. Still more often, your adversary's witness will
furnish a potential source of cumulative evidence corrobo-
rating the evidence of your own witnesses.

Tactical considerations will help you to determine
whether to open a new subject on cross-examination. Will
the answers of the witness be favorable to your client or lay
the predicate for effective impeachment of your adversary's
witnesses? Is it a subject that, though producing answers
favorable to you, may lead to other inquiries producing
unfavorable answers? Will the testimony on the subject as a
whole be of more harm than benefit to your case? Will
opening the matter possibly furnish proof for your adversary
that he omitted, either from hesitancy about inquiring into
the subject or from oversight? The competent arbitration
advocate views his immediate problem as an aspect of the
most effective presentation of the entire case. He is willing
to sacrifice any temporary triumph that is inconsistent with
that emphasis. It follows that although advantages to be
gained by opening new subjects on cross-examination are
obvious, you should observe some tactical limitations on
using them.

As with surprise questions to your own witness on
direct examination, there is a major risk of unfavorable
answers. In cross-examination, is the risk less serious because an unfavorable answer from your adversary's witness
does not make as great an impact? Or is the risk more
serious in that the witness, particularly if unfriendly toward
you, is more likely to answer unfavorably in both manner
and substance? If you can anticipate well before the hearing

that your adversary will use the witness, you may reduce the risk greatly during your preparation, particularly in deciding what questions not to ask. Yet often you will be able to think of new matters to ask about with confidence about what the witness will answer, and new questions for which the witness has not been prepared by your adversary. Working such virgin soil is one of the most fruitful and delightful phases of cross-examination.

Usually you will gain little by extending your new inquiries to matters irrelevant to the issues in your case or to questions of bias, interest, corruption, skill, or sources of knowledge of the witness. Arbitrators generally will not permit impeachment on collateral matters.

Asking for Repetition and Added Details

Neophyte arbitration advocates have a natural tendency to ask a witness on cross-examination to repeat testimony given on direct, interspersing here and there a few calls for more details. This procedure comes naturally to those who feel a need to cross-examine but have no specific goal or plan. Though occasionally the hope that some inconsistency will develop is realized, usually such cross-examination serves only to emphasize and strengthen the direct testimony. Do not follow this procedure without a specific aim and a reasonable basis for supposing that you may realize an advantage.

When you have evidence of contradiction or inconsistencies between the witness's testimony on direct examination and his previous statements, your first step in using such evidence effectively is to lay a firm foundation for its use, such that the witness cannot formulate a plausible explanation of the apparent inconsistency. In framing the questions, attempt to anticipate each possible excuse or explanation and get the witness committed to a contrary position before you point up the inconsistency. Otherwise, an apparently plausible excuse conceived by the witness may not only rob you of effective impeachment but will also make the net effect of your cross-examination worse than none.

This first step is essential even if you propose to offer the impeaching evidence independently rather than on cross-examination. Although the cross-examination in which you make the more detailed inquiries and call upon the witness to repeat and confirm his position serves temporarily to emphasize and not to weaken the witness's testimony, this is part of your larger plan of earning greater emphasis for the impeaching evidence when you offer it later. With sufficient emphasis the impeachment on one point may cast suspicion on the witness personally and thus on everything the witness has said. When you are using cross-examination for this purpose, however, it is generally not advisable to ask the witness to repeat his entire story or most of it; rather, single out the points on which you have impeaching evidence available and develop only them.

Shifting the Subject of Inquiry

The theory of the hop, skip, and jump method of cross-examination—shifting the subject of inquiry suddenly and frequently—is that the witness is kept so busy shifting his thought processes that he has no time to formulate dishonest answers, and those he does formulate, if he does so, will be so artless that you will be able to expose them. In practice, this method generally does not work. The arbitrator may have the same difficulty as the witness in shifting thought processes. In fact the arbitrator may have greater difficulty because he may be less familiar at that point in the hearing with the background of the case. Furthermore, if you catch the witness in some inconsistency, the arbitrator may be more likely to accept the excuse that the witness did not understand your questions than if you asked your questions in a logical pattern.

Using "Why" Questions

When an adverse witness takes an unreasonable position, you may have to repress an urge to ask "are you crazy?"; you may also be tempted to ask him "why?" Both questions are equally impractical. Probably (though not necessarily) the witness is sympathetic to the party who called him. With proper questioning, however, you can limit his opportunity to help that side by framing questions that hold him to facts. The question "why" opens the door to an explanation which may be not only responsive but also argumentative. In short, the "why" question removes barriers of inadmissibility. It allows the witness to state opinions, arguments, or inadmissible facts. Though an arbitrator might permit you to interrupt the answer to restrict the witness to matter that is not subject to exclusion, your interruption of a responsive answer may be as damaging as the answer itself.

The temptation to ask the "why" question is based upon the assumption that the witness has no explanation that would seem reasonable to you or to the arbitrator. There is, of course, that possibility, but the risk of harm if you are wrong is so great that it is a sound rule of thumb never to ask a "why" question.

Using Argumentative Questions

Some advocates in cross-examination regularly use the opportunity to recite their own theory of the case, barely nodding toward the theoretical purpose of cross-examination by introducing their statement with the phrase, "Isn't it a fact that. . . ." Though this may have some tactical value in helping the arbiter to understand and remember the advocate's position, it is a crude way of doing what generally can be done more effectively through other means. Long before cross-examination you have ample opportunity to present your theory of the case to the arbitrator at times without having to phrase the theory in the form of a question. Perhaps there is value in repeating your theory as often as possible. Bear in mind, however, that the arbitrator does realize that only what the witnesses say is evidence. Only to the extent that you can get answers from the witness that support your theory of the case, or help to impeach some part of your adversary's case, are you justified in continuing cross-examination; using cross-examination to state your theories is more likely to be detrimental than beneficial to your case.

This is not to say that you should never use an "Isn't it a fact that . . ." question. Frequently this form of question is

the best way of committing the witness in a way such that
the arbitrator realizes it clearly. Particularly is this so when
the question is one that the witness should be expected to
answer affirmatively.

If the witness is argumentative, something more can be
said for arguing with him a little, although most labor relations advocates would advise you not to do that. A well-
turned question is a better argument than a statement. The
ideal is to bait the argumentative witness enough that the
arbitrator will get the idea that he is arguing with you while
you are simply trying to get him to answer some questions
of fact. Furthermore, the argumentative witness is one you
may catch in an untenable extreme.

Demanding Clear Answers

A witness will often frame a seemingly implausible evasion
of a single question. One of your very important tasks as
cross-examiner is instant analysis of the evasive answer so
that you may follow up with further inquiries that pin down
the witness to one position or another on material questions. Requiring a clear answer not only produces this type
of testimony, it can also reveal the witness's bias or his
efforts to conceal relevant facts.

In determining how far to press an evasive witness for
a clear answer, consider the materiality of the first question
asked, the nature of the answer that the witness will probably give if forced to a showdown, and the probable reason
for the witness's reluctance to answer directly. If the original question is not important, the principal possibility of an
advantage from pressing the witness is to demonstrate his
reluctance to answer your questions frankly. It is not likely
that you can do this through questioning on a relatively
unimportant topic, except to the extent that this may contribute toward an overall impression of evasiveness if the
witness reacts similarly to other questions.

The mere fact that the witness is evading your question
on an important subject does not conclusively demonstrate
that you should press him on the matter. If the evasion is
apparent, you have already gained some advantage from it

because of the unfavorable reflection on the reliability of the witness's testimony. You may lose this advantage and suffer even more harm if you press a witness whose evasion is caused by something other than a desire to hurt your case or favor your opponent's case. The answer when finally extracted may be unfavorable to you.

If the risk of an explanation harmful to your case seems slight and worth taking, how should you press the witness for an answer? Make your questions simple and pointed. Break down and attack item by item any qualified or conditional answers so that you eliminate, or at least minimize, the opportunities for plausible evasion. If in the face of a simplified question the witness is still evasive, you may decide to drop the matter, because the evasion has effectively been brought to the attention of the arbitrator.

Should you ask the arbitrator to instruct the witness to answer the question? Such instruction usually produces an answer, but the witness cannot be required to answer a question that he does not understand or know the answer to; nor can he be required to give a categorical yes or no answer without explanation if such an answer would be inaccurate or misleading. If you have asked a question that cannot be answered categorically, the arbitrator will deny your request for an instruction to the witness, probably to the detriment of your cross-examination generally. Although you may think that your question is not of this type, if there is room for doubt, it is generally better not to risk asking the arbitrator for an instruction to the witness.

Responding to Questions from the Witness

Occasionally a witness will ask you a question as you are cross-examining him. If the question is one seeking an explanation or clarification of the question you have asked him, readily give any explanation necessary to make your question clear and unambiguous. Any other attitude on your part may make your cross-examination look more like a game than a search for the truth. If the witness's question is rhetorical or argumentative—and usually such questions will be tacked on the end of the witness's answer to a question of yours—the problem is more difficult. In preparing the case you have considered all contentions that you think might be raised by your adversary and all questions that he might be expected to ask of any of your witnesses. Usually, therefore, you will have at the tip of your tongue an answer that at least seems to you to be logical and convincing. And you do not want to appear to the arbitrator to be evading an embarrassing question. On the other hand, answering the witness may encourage more questions from him and more interruptions and interference with the direction and purpose of your cross-examination. You have a great advantage over the witness in the privilege of asking questions while he must give only answers—you should not surrender that advantage lightly.

Discrediting Testimony of Other Witnesses

Testimony may be discredited by independent evidence from other sources as well as by cross-examination of the witnesses who gave it.

Whatever its nature, independent proof used to discredit testimony of a witness is more effective if it comes from witnesses your adversary calls rather than those you call. If the difference is only in degrees of certainty and emphasis, you will usually profit by bolstering the testimony of your own witness with admissions from a witness your adversary has called. On the other hand, if the differences are more substantial, your decision on whether to go into the subject with the adverse witness must depend upon your appraisal of how the arbitrator reacted to your witness's testimony alone. Ordinarily it will be advisable for you to cross-examine on any subject which you expect your adversary may refer to later. The risk of unfavorable testimony, as to both substance and form of expression, is greater if your adversary has time to confer with the witness and prepare him for specific inquiries than if you cross-examine him before such preparation.

Inquiring into Opportunity to Observe

Proof of poor opportunity for observation is a customary method of discrediting testimony; ability to observe in the sense of personal capacity is less often an issue. Whether you should cross-examine on poor opportunity or ability in particular instances will depend on the principal purpose of your cross-examination and the contribution of this method to the total effect of the cross-examination.

Will the effort to show poor opportunity to observe be effective? Cross-examination is dangerous if it merely re-inforces the direct testimony, because the witness is not subject to effective attack on this ground. You may be able to discredit him by committing him to an extreme position that is either patently absurd or clearly inconsistent with the actual circumstances as proved by other evidence. On the other hand, if the actual circumstances reveal that the wit-ness had a reasonably good opportunity for observation, the fact that the witness is inclined to be conservative in his statement—he is the type who will say only that the horse was white on the side he saw and not that it was a white horse—does not necessarily imply that he should be cross-examined on his opportunity to observe. The effect may be only to reinforce your adversary's argument that the witness was entirely disinterested and careful to be fair and accurate in everything he told the arbitrator.

Moreover, if, for example, your primary purpose in cross-examination is to develop evidence favorable to you on a subject not touched on in the direct examination, proof of poor opportunity to observe might have the inci-dental effect of casting doubt on the other subject on which the witness gives testimony favorable to you. Weigh the advantages of weakening the adverse testimony against the disadvantages of weakening the favorable testimony. If the favorable effect of the testimony on the new subject has been striking, the total effect of the cross-examination may be weakened by a showing of even doubtful opportunity to observe.

Proving Bad Character

Evidence of the bad character of a witness may bear directly on the issues of the case, but more often it is admissible merely on the theory that it affects the credibility of the witness. An arbitrator's sense of justice will often make him uncomfortable with apparent mudslinging regarding matters not properly before him for decision. Of course, the character of every witness is an issue to some extent because it affects the credibility of his testimony. Arbitrators, however, do not necessarily agree that any evidence of bad character that is admissible is material. They may regard the use of such evidence as unfair and may consciously or subconsciously weigh that factor against the party offering the evidence. It is therefore usually inadvisable to offer this type of evidence, unless it is clearly admissible; even then, consider carefully whether the arbitrator will regard the evidence as bearing closely enough on the credibility of the witness's testimony in the particular case that its use is justified.

The decision as to whether to use such evidence, therefore, involves an appraisal of how directly the evidence bears on the credibility of the witness and the attitude the arbitrator has brought with him into the hearing.

Objections to the Form of Questions

Every advocate asks some improperly leading questions, inadvertently if not by design. With some adversaries you could use up an enormous amount of time objecting. Yet obviously if you do not object, your adversary may succeed in leading the witness into testimony much more favorable to him than otherwise would have been allowed. Your objection also serves to call to the attention of the arbitrator the unfairness of the method your adversary is using to obtain favorable testimony. But the major vices of the leading question—coaching the witness and getting something before the arbitrator that he might not otherwise hear—are already accomplished before you can object. Your reasons for objecting, then, are not so much related to exclude the anticipated answer as to restrain the use of further leading questions and call to the arbitrator's attention the use already made and its bearing on the credibility of the evidence.

If an adversary persists in asking leading questions, the generally preferred practice is not to object to every question, but to call the matter to the attention of the arbitrator by periodically pointing out the practice and asking that the arbitrator be allowed to hear the witness tell his own story. If the practice is persistent, you may also request an instruction by the arbitrator that your adversary not lead the witness.

It is also sometimes wise to object to questions on the ground of form if a question calls for an answer regarding knowledge as a preliminary fact supporting admissibility. For example, when a witness is asked to state whether he is familiar with the custom regarding a specific matter, he usually replies by stating what he thinks the custom to be rather than answering yes or no to the question. If you consider that there is reasonable hope of getting the witness to admit that he is not familiar generally with the practices of others, but only with the practices of a few individuals— so that his idea of the custom is based upon insufficient knowledge—object or else move that the arbitrator instruct the witness to answer the question only yes or no. If, on the other hand, you know that the witness will testify so as to qualify himself, your objection or request for the instruction, though sustained, would serve no purpose. It would be better instead to develop by cross-examination any weakness in the degree of familiarity of the witness with the custom.

Final Argument

The scope of final argument is limited by the factual and contract law issues in the case. The resolution of conflicts in the evidence usually depends in some measure on reasonable inferences, deductions, and conclusions. These may be offered to the arbitrator in final argument; sometimes the inferences and deductions are afforded greater weight than the testimony of witnesses.

The bulk of the argument will, of course, relate to the evidence and exhibits in the case and the inferences, deductions, and conclusions which may be drawn therefrom.

These constitute the principal working material in every case. Absence of evidence or failure of proof from an adversary is also a proper subject.

In some cases the conduct of the parties, as proved by the evidence, is a particularly noteworthy subject for final argument, as, for example, where a party has been deceptive, inconsistent, or contradictory in the assertion of his claim or defense.

So, too, comment may properly be made about the fact that a party has failed to produce evidence or testimony—books, records, or other exhibits—under his control or available to him.

The credibility of witnesses may always be discussed in final argument. However, vituperative or inflammatory language should never be used, in this context or any other.

Not only may the credibility of the opponent's witnesses be attacked, but the credibility of one's own witnesses may also be urged, by references both to the reasonableness of the testimony and to the support which it receives from other evidence.

The advocate may properly refer to contract law and relevant precedent, relating the evidence to the pertinent authority.

Clearly, final argument can only be effective if the advocate has closely observed and absorbed all developments throughout the entire course of the hearing.

Proper presentation (incorporating familiarity with all aspects of the case, the contract, and the evidence), review of opposing testimony as well as your own, and simplification of the issues will reduce the controlling issues to a minimum. Here the argument should be directed. If there is a single controlling question in the case, confine the argument to that issue.

Most cases will have strong and weak points on both sides. Not only should one's own strong points be emphasized but those of the opponent should be dealt with. And while the opponent's weaknesses should be stressed, one's own should not be ignored.

The strength of the opponent's case should be recognized even though not expressly acknowledged, and an attack should ordinarily be directed at it. Similarly, weak phases of one's own case should ordinarily be bolstered by all the implications which the evidence affords. If you fail to do this, your opponent will be quick to take advantage.

But if satisfactory arguments are not available, either by direct attack or by confession and avoidance, the opponent's strong points or one's own weaknesses are better treated lightly or not at all. Argument which is unconvincing only emphasizes the things that hurt.

In view of the tricks that memory plays, it is well to support a statement, in final argument, by a written memorandum. Your notes in the course of the trial recording statements of an opposing advocate or the testimony of witnesses may be used effectively. There is an obvious psychological advantage in being able to say, in effect, "I made a note of what the opposing advocate said in his opening statement on this subject; let me read it to you."

Written exhibits should be read whenever they contain material bearing directly upon the principal issues in the case—whether they support your own position or challenge the other side's.

There is also truth as well as quaintness in the proverb that one picture is worth a thousand words. The use of drawings, charts, photographs, or other visual evidence is very effective in final argument. Demonstrating how a machine works or how an accident happened, outlining the boundaries of a department or factory by the use of exhibits will very often get the point across more effectively than mere words.

8
Principles and Practices

The Moving Party

In all but discipline cases, the union as the moving party, the one asserting a claim, should make at least an introductory presentation. In most cases, the union is expected to present its whole case before the company does so, because the party with the substantive burden of proof—whether in a court of law, an arbitration proceeding, or a grievance procedure—has the task of presenting the initial evidence. The union must establish that a contract violation has occurred. If it establishes what is called a prima facie case (defined as support of the complainant's contentions by evidence, that, if believed, would sustain those contentions), the employer must rebut that evidence.

As we have said, in most cases the complaining party is the union. However, it seems a well-established tenet of labor relations that the burden of proof in discipline or discharge disputes must be carried by the party who initiated the challenged action; the employer is, therefore, called on to establish the facts it asserts as the basis for having taken presumably positive corrective action. In such cases the employer must present its position first, and it also has the right to close the hearing with a position statement. This procedure may of course be altered or waived by agreement of the parties.

The Burden of Proof

One purpose of the labor agreement is to promote favorable relations between the company and its employees. To

161

achieve this, management must under its contract always make a fair and proper determination of the facts involved in any discipline or discharge action it takes. It must stand ready to support its allegations against employees charged with improper conduct.

Arbitrators differ on the quantity and quality of proof demanded from the employer. Some require that guilt be established "beyond reasonable doubt," as do our criminal courts. Labor arbitrators are inclined to impose this measurement when the charges are by nature criminal, or involve substantial injury to the employee's work status, job security, or reputation. Others see the burden of proof as carried if a "preponderance of the evidence" establishes a prima facie case. Here the burden of proof may actually transfer from one party to the other during the arbitration proceedings. An example will illustrate this.

Imagine that a firm has discharged an employee for incompetence. To support its action, it presents evidence of poor-quality materials, bad parts, and a low productivity record. It establishes that the employee is in fact the offender, and it shows that the corrective action was appropriate to his act of misconduct and his record. This evidence constitutes a prima facie case.

However, the union alleges that the poor work was not the product of the discharged employee and that his low productivity was the result of some factors beyond his control. At this point, the burden of proof transfers to the union; it cannot establish its claim merely by stating it, any more than the employer can, but must present evidence in support of the employee's innocence. If it does so, then the burden of proof transfers again, back to the employer.

Evidence—Arbitral Treatment

Legal rules of evidence are not commonly observed strictly in the arbitration process, unless required by both parties; this is infrequent.[1] Furthermore, American Arbitration Association Rule 28 states: "The arbitrator shall be the judge of the relevance and materiality of the evidence offered and conformity to legal rules of evidence shall not be necessary."[2]

Arbitrator W. Willard Wirtz, Secretary of Labor under Presidents Kennedy and Johnson, has observed:

> Arbitrators have established the pattern of ordered informality; performing major surgery on the legal rules of evidence and procedure but retaining the good sense of these rules; greatly simplifying but not eliminating the hearsay and parol evidence rules; taking the rules for the admissibility of evidence and remolding them into rules for weighing it; striking the fat but saving the heart of the practices of cross-examination, presumptions, burden of proof, and the like.[3]

What this comes down to is that in the great majority of cases, "any evidence, information, or testimony is acceptable which is pertinent to the case and which helps the arbitrator to understand and decide the problem before him."[4]

The liberal introduction of evidence by arbitrators has its share of critics, most of them lawyers. Lawyers have an instinctive aversion to the arbitrator's attitude: "Well, I am not sure myself about its relevance but I will take it for what it is worth." However, Harry Shulman, late expert in arbitration, commented that "the more serious danger is not that the arbitrator will hear too much irrelevancy, but rather that he will not hear enough of the relevant."[5]

Arbitrator William E. Simkin, one-time national director of the Federal Mediation and Conciliation Service (FMCS), dwelt for a moment on the cathartic effect of the liberal acceptance of evidence:

> One of the fundamental purposes of an arbitration hearing is to let people get things off their chest, regardless of the decision. The arbitration proceeding is the opportunity for a third party, an outside party, to come in and act as a sort of father confessor to the parties, to let them get rid of their troubles, get them out in the open, and have a feeling of someone hearing their troubles. Because I believe so strongly that that is

one of the fundamental purposes of arbitration, I don't think you ought to use any rules of evidence. You have to make up your own mind as to what is pertinent or not in the case. Lots of times I have let people talk for five minutes, when I knew all the time that they were talking it had absolutely nothing to do with the case — just completely foreign to it. But there was a fellow testifying, either as a worker or a company representative, who had something that was important for him to get rid of. It was a good time for him to get rid of it.[6]

The point of course, is that, in the overwhelming majority of cases, arbitrators are receptive to almost any type of evidence the parties may wish to submit. What may not appear to be particularly germane at the outset may later be found intrinsic to the issue. It is not uncommon for arbitrators to accept evidence "for what it is worth," reserving their opinion of, and reactions to, the questionable evidence until they have had an opportunity to evaluate it against the record. Then, if in their judgment it is not sufficiently relevant to the issue at hand, they accord it no weight in their final determinations. Unless an arbitration statute requires explicit adherence to legal rules of evidence, the strict observance of legal rules of evidence is customarily not necessary.

Best Evidence

The wisest rule is always to use the best evidence available. Eyewitness accounts provide more compelling testimony than hearsay; testimony that an employee was not at work will be more conclusive if it is supported by payroll and production records.

Arbitrators look askance at evidence from the employer about events that occur after a discharge action. In determining whether the action taken by the company fits the accusation against the employee, arbitrators are concerned only with the employee's conduct preceding the discharge.

It is unwise to hold back records and information germane to the grievance issue. If time cards, production records, absenteeism reports, payroll records, prior grievance or arbitration settlements, and the like are available, they should be introduced. To be of maximum effectiveness, such information should have been made available to the other party preceding the arbitration hearing, preferably during the earlier stages of the grievance procedure.

Examples—Real Evidence

1. absenteeism records
2. production records
3. payroll records
4. time cards
5. discipline record(s)
6. tardiness records
7. prior arbitration decisions
8. prior grievance settlements
9. photographs
10. tangible—physical materials

Circumstantial Evidence

Circumstantial evidence is regarded with caution by arbitrators, just as it is by the courts. To be decisive such evidence should preclude any reasonable hypothesis other than that which it purports to establish. Such evidence, though common in arbitration proceedings, is generally a last resort. It consists of an accumulation of peripheral events or conditions that, taken together, reasonably point to the fact.

At the Stockham Pipe Fitting Company, circumstantial evidence was sufficiently persuasive to uphold a discharge action in a dispute over the discharge of employees for instigating an unauthorized work stoppage. Arbiter Whitley P. McCoy evaluated the web of circumstances surrounding the matter:

> Because of the secret nature of the offense of these men, proof is extremely difficult. It does not follow from this that proof may be dispensed with or that

mere suspicious circumstances may take the place of proof, as I have indicated in sustaining the grievances of four men. But I think it does follow that something less than the most direct and most positive proof is sufficient; in other words, that, just as in cases of fraud and conspiracy, legitimate inferences may be drawn from such circumstances as a prior knowledge of the time set for the strike. Unusual actions were evident in circulating among the employees just prior to 9:30, communication of the time set to employees, and signals however surreptitious, given at that hour. Mere prior guilty knowledge of the time set would not alone be sufficient since presumably many of the employees must have been told the time a half-hour, an hour, or several hours in advance. Nor would merely being the first in a department to quit at the stroke of 9:30, standing alone, be sufficient. A wave of the hand, which might as reasonably be interpreted as a signal of good-bye as a signal to others to go out, as in the case of Hollingsworth, would of itself be insufficient. But these or other suspicious circumstances, in combination, and especially in case of known leaders in the Union's affairs, may be sufficient to convince the reasonable mind of guilt.[7]

The opinion of the majority of arbitrators is that circumstantial evidence is real evidence, providing every other possible explanation is eliminated. Long experience has also taught that circumstantial evidence may sometimes be more persuasive than direct evidence. However, arbitrators remain understandably cautious.

In deciding a dispute between the Illinois Bell Telephone Company and the International Brotherhood of Electrical Workers, Arbitrator Meyer S. Ryder discussed the standards of proof to be used when circumstantial evidence is involved:

The Chairman holds that in discharge matters where the employee offense being treated with carries along with it connotations of corruption and illegality, were the employee to be held guilty of the offense, the standard of evidentiary proof to convict should be no real subjective question of guilt in the minds of him or those who have to decide. Acceptable to this proposition should be evidence of circumstances or combination of circumstances such as leave no doubt that what is indicated is actually present. Should it be considered that the application of standards of proof in a criminal proceeding under the law go beyond and are greater than these standards, then the criminal law standards should not be held to apply in an industrial relations arbitration proceeding. Accordingly, the Chairman has applied the standards he has enunciated above to the discharge matters.[8]

Arbitrator Paul M. Herbert has commented that the use of circumstantial evidence "does not eliminate in any sense the requirement that there must be a clear and convincing proof to establish that the offense charged was committed."[9] It has also been said that mere suspicion is not sufficient to establish a wrongdoing.[10]

Putting it still another way, Arbitrator Clair V. Duff has stated:

> [The arbitrator] must exercise extreme care so that by due deliberation and careful judgment he may avoid making hasty or false deductions. If the evidence producing the chain of circumstances pointing to guilt is weak and inconclusive, no probability of fact may be inferred from the combined circumstances.[11]

Hearsay

"Hearsay evidence" is the narration by one person of matters told him by another. Hearsay evidence is usually barred in legal proceedings because it cannot be tested through cross-examination. A written communication may also be categorized as "hearsay"; and the fact that a hearsay statement is reduced to writing does not render it admissible. Obviously, it is as impossible to cross-examine a written document as it is an absent third party.

Arbitrators generally reject hearsay evidence when it is properly objected to. The reasons are self-evident—the contesting party has no chance to confront or cross-examine the alleged witness. Hearsay testimony may be motivated by self-interest, malice, or spite. It may be the misrepresentation of an irresponsible person or it may be partially or totally fabricated.

But arbitrators, not bound by strict legal rules of evidence, do admit hearsay evidence, and weigh it in the light of the lack of opportunity to cross-examine. For example, Arbitrator Harold I. Elbert has ruled that, although they may be hearsay, doctors' certificates are admissible in an arbitration proceeding as proof of an employee's illness; in fact, medical certificates are commonly admitted in evidence and given weight by arbitrators in determining whether an employee was sick.[12]

Arbitrator Benjamin Aaron has analyzed the weight to be accorded hearsay evidence:

> A competent arbitrator may be depended upon substantially to discount some kinds of hearsay evidence that he has admitted over objection. He will do so selectively, however, and not on the assumption that hearsay evidence, as such, is not to be credited. If, for example, a newly appointed personnel manager, or a recently elected business agent, offers a letter to his predecessor from a third party, the arbitrator is likely to ignore the fact that the evidence is hearsay; if satisfied that the document is genuine, he will give it such weight as its relevancy dictates. On the other hand, hearsay testimony about statements allegedly made by "the boys in the shop" or by executives "in the front office," though perhaps not excluded from the record by the arbitrator, probably will have no effect on his decision.[13]

Another arbitrator, Arthur R. Lewis, has commented that "the reasons calling for the existence of a hearsay rule in common-law jury actions should at least guide the judgment of the arbitrator in the evaluation of the weight, if any, to be attributed to such evidence in an arbitration proceeding."[14] In any case, it is extremely unlikely that an arbitrator will decide an issue with a ruling based on and supported by hearsay evidence alone. It is worth noting that the AAA rules allow the arbitrator to consider the evidence of witnesses by written document, but recommend that it should be given only the weight to which it is deemed to be entitled after consideration of any objection made regarding its admission.

Thus, in arbitration, hearsay evidence is admissible "for what it is worth." The "for what it is worth" rule is not a satisfactory yardstick but it is a compromise between two extremes which are often more unsatisfactory.

The principal witness, however, should not attempt to relate alleged facts as told to him unless there is no other way of getting them into evidence. If the facts are worth putting in the record, let the foreman, personnel manager, complainant, or grieving employee, the person with first-hand knowledge, tell his own story if the facts are not admitted by the adversary or unless they can be better proved by authentic records or documents. Prove your case by the best and most authentic evidence available to you.

The basic objection to hearsay is that it gives the adversary no opportunity to cross-examine the person who is quoted (and perhaps misquoted), and thus amounts to the taking of an unfair advantage. In courts of law it is inadmissible, unless there are circumstances which are deemed sufficient to substitute for the oath and cross-examination, and unless it consequently falls under one of the many exceptions to the rule.

Parol Evidence Rule

It has long been a substantive rule of law that in the absence of fraud or mutual mistake, oral statements are not admissible to modify, vary, explain, or contradict the plain terms of a valid written contract.

The rule has many ramifications. In arbitration it is

seldom referred to by its name, but all parties should keep in mind that there is a very sound basis for the rule. To allow oral statements made during contract negotiations to modify or contradict the plain language finally adopted could throw the best written contract into doubt. Where a contract is plain and unambiguous, oral statements or reservations made by either party do not change it.

If the terms of the contract are ambiguous or clearly susceptible to more than one meaning, then parol evidence is admissible to show what the parties meant at the time of making the contract. The rule seldom comes into arbitration under that heading, for it is more tactful for the objector to simply point out the unreliability of the claimed oral agreement based on no more than faulty memories, especially when it conflicts with the written version.

Objections to Evidence

Each party is entitled to object when it believes the other party is seeking to introduce improper evidence or argument. Such objections, when based upon some plausible grounds, can serve a useful function even if overruled, for the arbitrator will have been cautioned to examine the challenged material more closely before giving it weight. A party is also entitled to object to evidence he considers irrelevant, for the record should not be burdened with material having little or no bearing.

However, objections which have no plausible basis, and those which are repetitious, should be avoided, as has been advised by Arbitrator Clarence M. Updegraff:

> Do not make captious, whimsical, or unnecessary objections to testimony or arguments of the other party. Such interruptions are likely to waste time and confuse issues. The arbitrator, no doubt, will realize without having the matter expressly mentioned more than once, when he is hearing weak testimony such as hearsay and immaterial statements.[15]

Offers of Compromise Inadmissible

The purpose of the contractual grievance machinery is to provide an instrument by which the parties may seek remedies to problems between them. To maintain its functional purpose, such machinery must be used in an open and uninhibited way. If everyone's needs are to be served, each party must feel free to search for accommodation or negotiate compromises. Each must be free of fear that if his offers are refused, it will not be be interpreted as a sign of weakness by an arbitrator.

For this reason, arbitrators give little, if any, weight to revelations of previous offers. The logic of this attitude is sound. One arbitrator put it succinctly:

> It is clear that any offer made by either party during the course of conciliation cannot prejudice that party's case when the case comes to arbitration. It is the very essence of conciliation that compromise proposals will go further than a party may consider itself bound to go on a strict interpretation of its rights.

For instance, upon returning to work after a back injury, an employee had refused, on the advice of the union, to consult yet another doctor, after having submitted to examinations by the employer's doctor and a clinic. Arbitrator John Sembower ruled that the evidence of that refusal had to be disregarded. The arbitration was dealing with a dispute involving the employer's refusal to reinstate the employee. It appeared to Sembower that the final medical examination was part of an attempt to settle the grievance before arbitrating it. As such, he held that the parties' attempts to resolve their differences should not be allowed to prejudice their positions at arbitration. If proposals, counterproposals, and offers of compromise could be seized upon and used later in arbitration against a party, the result would be to throttle the dispute-settling efficiency of the grievance machinery.

The "De Minimis" Rule

In denying grievance, arbitrators sometimes apply the rule of *de minimis con curat lex,* under which trifling or immaterial matters will not be taken into account. Often in applying this principle the arbitrator concludes that the action complained of is such a slight departure from what is generally required by the agreement that the action must be viewed either as a permissible exception or as not constituting an injury at all. The de minimis concept has sometimes been applied, for example, in denying grievances protesting the performance by management personnel of small amounts of bargaining unit work where a unit employee was not readily available.

Application of the de minimis rule has been rejected where "the amount has been small but the principle large." And, in any event, Arbitrator Harold W. Davey has explained that no hard and fast mathematical line can be drawn between minimal on the one hand and substantial on the other, but that each case should be decided in terms of its own circumstances.

Weight and Credibility of the Evidence

It is within the province of the arbitrator to determine the weight, relevancy, and authenticity of evidence. The general approach of arbitrators is effectively illustrated by Arbitrator George Cheney. In reviewing the discharge of an employee, he noted that the case illustrated a type of situation where the facts are to a large extent determined by the weight and credibility accorded to the testimony of the witnesses and to the documentary evidence offered by the parties. He pointed out that, in arriving at the truth in such a case, an arbitrator must consider whether conflicting statements ring true or false; that he will note the witnesses' demeanor while on the stand; and that he will credit or discredit testimony according to his impressions of the witnesses' veracity. Arbitrator Cheney also pointed out that, in determining where the preponderance of the evidence lies with respect to any material point, the arbitrator will take into consideration whether the witness speaks from first-hand information or whether his testimony is largely based on hearsay or gossip. In summarizing, Arbitrator Cheney stated that the duty of the arbitrator is simply to determine the truth respecting material matters in controversy, as he believes it to be. The arbitrator bases his decision upon a full and fair consideration of the entire evidence, after he has accorded each witness and each piece of documentary evidence, the weight, if any, to which he honestly believes it to be entitled.[16]

Arbitrator Clair V. Duff, in turn, has offered some considerations relevant in evaluating testimony:

Any attempt to sort credible testimony from that which is not worthy of belief is very difficult for at least four basic reasons. They may be briefly stated:

INTEREST. While having an interest or stake in the outcome does not disqualify a witness, it renders his testimony subject to most careful scrutiny.... Few witnesses will deliberately falsify but there is a common tendency to "put your best foot forward." This tendency, either consciously or subconsciously, leads many witnesses to remember and express testimony in a way favorable to the result which they hope the Hearing will produce.

PERCEPTION. Frequently the initial observation is faulty or incomplete because the observer has no prior knowledge that a dispute will develop concerning what he has seen or heard and his casual sensory impression is not sharp and keen.

MEMORY. The remembrance of an event weeks or months after it occurred is frequently dim and inaccurate and a witness may be confused as to facts which initially he correctly perceived. By lapse of time precise details may elude his memory.

COMMUNICATION. The manner in which a witness expresses what he saw and heard may fail to communicate exactly his initial perception of the occurrence, so that after listening to the testimony and the cross-examination of the witnesses, the fact-finder may not have had transmitted to him a completely accurate impression of the facts, even though they were initially observed carefully and well remembered by the witness.[17]

Arbitrator Joseph Rosenfarb cautioned that while "both sides might be subject to the unconscious influences of self-interest, personal predilection, or antipathy," it is the duty of the arbitrator "to examine the testimony of each witness on its own merits." Arbitrator Samuel Krimsly has cautioned that if a grievant's testimony "is colored by bias," employees used as company witnesses may, like union members, have "a bias by reason of their employment."[18]

Where the testimony is highly contradictory, it ordinarily "becomes incumbent upon the Arbitrator to sift and evaluate the testimony to the best of his ability, and reach the best conclusion he can as to the actual fact situation."[18] However, sometimes "it is unnecessary to resolve the substantial conflict in the evidence to obtain an unobstructed view of the scene. By piecing together the parts, the broad outlines of the whole picture emerges." As Arbitrator R. W. Fleming has aptly observed:

> Arbitrators are not equipped with any special divining rod which enables them to know who is telling the truth and who is not where a conflict in testimony develops. They can only do what the courts have done in similar circumstances for centuries. A judgment must finally be made, and there is a possibility that the judgment when made is wrong.[19]

Time Limitations

Promptness is one of the most important aspects of grievance settlement. All parties agree that promptness in the settlement of grievances leads to better labor-management relationships; opinion differs, however, as to the best means of insuring such promptness. Many agreements provide time limits for taking complaints to the grievance procedure as well as time limits for processing grievances through the various steps of the procedure; others do not. Some parties feel that time limits provide a safeguard against stalling and against the accumulations of cases and pressing of stale claims.

In the final analysis, prompt settlement of grievances depends, not upon the presence of contractual time limits, but upon a sincere desire of the parties to settle differences. That time limits do have definite value, however, may be presumed from the fact that numerous agreements contain them. Without question, such limits provide an additional element of order to the grievance procedure.

No set formula is available for establishing time limits; they will depend on the special circumstances of the parties. The agreement may fix time limits for each step of the procedure, or an over-all time limit for complete processing of a grievance, or simply forbid delay. Any of these might be coupled with a time limit for the initial submission of grievances. Different limits may be prescribed for the submission of different types of grievances, as perhaps a 5-day limit for filing discharge and pay adjustment disputes, and a 30-day limit for all other grievances.

Some cases hold there is no time limit for filing grievances where the agreement does not specify any. But some arbitrators have held that even though the contract does not state a time limit, a requirement for filing within a reasonable time is inferred by the establishment of a grievance procedure. It has also been held that where the contract states no time limit for filing grievances but does state specific time limits for taking grievances to the various steps of the procedure once they have been filed, the evident intent of the contract is that grievances must be filed with reasonable promptness.

Where the absence of strict time limits results in the acceptance of grievances notwithstanding delayed filing, the arbitrator may make the grievance adjustment retroactive only to the date on which the grievance was filed or to some other date short of full retroactivity. In particular, arbitrators can be expected to deny that part of a claim which, if allowed, would result in a loss to one party caused by the negligent delay of the other party in asserting the claim. Whether the arbitrator calls such delay laches, acquiescence, or "sleeping on one's rights," the principle appears to be generally applied.

If the agreement does contain clear time limits for filing and prosecuting grievances, failure to observe them generally will result in dismissal of the grievance if the failure is protested. Thus the practical effect of late filing in many instances is that the merits of the dispute are never decided.

It has been held that doubts as to the interpretation of contractual time limits or as to whether they have been met should be resolved against forfeiture of the right to process the grievance. Moreover, even if time limits are clear, late filing will not result in dismissal of the grievance if the circumstances are such that it would be unreasonable to require strict compliance.

If both parties have been lax about observing time limits in the past, an arbitrator will hesitate to enforce limits strictly unless there has been prior notice by a party of intent to demand strict adherence.

Of course time limits may be extended or waived by special written or even oral agreement. Even where an agreement expressly required time limit waivers to be in writing, it has been held that the parties' actions may produce a waiver without a writing.

In many cases time limits have been held waived by a party in negotiating a grievance without making clear and timely objection. But there are cases holding to the contrary. And where clear and timely objection is made to time limit violations, no waiver will result from subsequent processing of the grievance on the merits. Indeed, it has been suggested that upon making timely objection to delayed filing, the objecting party ordinarily should then discuss the grievance on the merits so that all issues will be ready for presentation to an arbitrator if the case reaches that stage. Under a less expeditious procedure the objecting party may refuse to entertain the grievance on the ground that it is null and void, forcing the grievant to file a second grievance involving the time issue alone; discussion of the original dispute on the merits would thus be delayed pending resolution of the time issue.

The contract provisions would appear to determine whether Saturdays, Sundays, holidays, and the day of the occurrence are to be counted in computing time. An arbitrator might be inclined toward flexibility in applying a short time limit within which a holiday falls, if the principle of prompt grievance processing is not seriously jeopardized.

Some agreements provide specifically that grievances are to be filed within a certain number of days after they "occur or are discovered." Even without such specific provision, arbitrators have held that one cannot be expected to file a grievance until he is aware or should be aware of the action upon which the grievance is based. But time limits "cannot be extended by the excuse that the grievant just didn't think of it sooner." Furthermore, where an employee had knowledge of adverse action but did not speak up, the time limit will not be extended because the union did not know.

A party sometimes announces its intention to do a given act which it does not do until later. Similarly, a party may do an act whose adverse effect upon another does not result until later. In some such situations arbitrators have held that for purposes of applying time limits the "occurrence" is at the later date. For example, where a company changed a seniority date on its records as a correction, a grievance protesting the change was held timely though not filed until nine months later; the arbitrator stated that the basis of the grievance would be the employee's frustrated attempt to exercise seniority rights based upon the old date, rather than the mere change in the company's records.

In this general connection, too, where a grievance protesting a layoff was filed seven days after the employee signed the layoff notice, the filing was held timely although the contract placed a five-day limit on filing grievances; two days were considered reasonable for the notice to reach the grievant. In another case the agreement required the company to answer a grievance within ten days, but the arbitrator refused to determine the allowed period on an "hour and minute" basis, where the parties had not previously applied their time limits so exactly. The arbitrator also stated that delivery of the answer to the U.S. mail was equivalent to delivery to the union. The combined effect of these two cases is that a time limit does not start running against a party until he is actually informed of the other party's position, and his response will be timely if it is thereafter deposited in the mails within the time limitation. This is consistent with the principle that doubts about the interpretation of contractual time limits should be resolved against forfeiture of grievances.

A party may sometimes be permitted to toll the running of time limits by giving notice to the other party of reasonable basis for delaying the filing of a grievance.

Many arbitrators have held that "continuing" violations of the agreement (as opposed to a single isolated and completed transaction) give rise to "continuing" grievances—each day there is a new "occurrence"; these arbitrators have permitted the filing of such grievances at any time (although any back pay ordinarily runs only from the date of filing). For example, where the agreement provided for filing "within 10 working days of the occurrence," it was held that where employees were erroneously denied work, each day lost was to be considered a new "occurrence" and that a grievance presented within 10 working days of any such day lost would be timely.

Sometimes an agreement will provide that any grievance not appealed from one step to the next within a specified time shall be considered settled on the basis of the last answer. On one occasion this type of provision was applied strictly, with the result that a grievance which, by error, had been left unappealed until the time limit had expired was held to have been settled.

If the foreman does not answer within the prescribed time, the grievant may take the complaint to the next step of the procedure. The failure of the foreman to answer will not be interpreted as an admission of the grievance by default (unless the agreement expressly calls for such default), since the burden is on the grievant to carry the complaint to the next step following the lapse of the specified time. But it has been emphasized that the foreman should make a decision or comment on each grievance.

CITATIONS

1. 10 LA 955.
2. 30 LA 1086.
3. Wirtz, Willard W. "Due Process of Arbitrations," The Arbitrator and the Parties 1, 13, BNA, 1958.
4. Simkin, Williams, and Kennedy, William. Arbitration of Grievances, Bulletin No. 82, p. 25, Wash: US Dept. of Labor, Div. of Stds., 1946.
5. Shulman. "Reason, Contract and Law in Labor Relations," Harvard Law Review 68 (1955): pp. 999, 1017.
6. Conference on Training of Law Students in Labor Relations, Vol. 3, Transcript of Proceeding, Harvard Law Review (1947), pp. 636–37.
7. 4 LA 744; 7 LA 239.
8. 39 LA 470; 45 LA 490; 40 LA 598.
9. 29 LA 604.
10. 19 LA 413.
11. 29 LA 718.
12. 29 LA 291; 20 LA 451; 19 LA 417.
13. Aaron, Benjamin. "Some Procedural Problems in Arbitration," Vanderbilt Law Review 10 (1957), pp. 733–44.
14. 16 LA 727.
15. 24 LA 430.
16. 23 LA 171.
17. 29 LA 718.
18. 43 LA 46.
19. 33 LA 25.

9
Conclusion

No one possesses all of the characteristics which make for the perfect arbitral advocate. Gifts of memory, ready wit, clarity of thought, facility of expression, grasp of figures, experience in business, technical knowledge, ability to simplify the complex, understanding of human psychology, physical stamina–these and other qualities are meted out to everyone in different measure. One thing that each person can do, however, is to review his efforts objectively and profit from his own mistakes and from the experience of others. Seldom has anyone ever tried a case so well that in retrospect he does not see some aspect which might have been better presented.

Retrospection is a useful guide to methods for trying the next case. The advocate who reviews every case, regardless of its outcome, testing what was done against established principles, who is not too readily discouraged by early failures nor too satisfied with early success, can, whether his gifts be great or small, achieve reasonable competence in the presentation of his future cases.

Until an advocate has mastered the technique of exploratory examination, he would be well advised to refrain from cross-examination unless he knows exactly where he is headed and approximately what he may expect to elicit. Unplanned cross-examination is rarely effective. There are times, of course, when it is essential in cross-examination to discredit a witness or his testimony even though no material for cross-examination was available in advance. At such times it may be necessary to resort to the dangerous and difficult exploratory cross-examination. Except for such a rare situation, however, cross-examination should follow a definite plan.

It is certainly unlikely that, under the impulse of the cross-examiner's questions, a witness who has deliberately told untruths will call for sackcloth and ashes, beat his breast in repentance, and confess that he has told a willful falsehood. It is sheer folly, therefore, to repeat questions substantially in the form in which they were asked on direct examination in the hope of stirring the conscience of the witness. The advocate who would be effective as a cross-examiner must always bear in mind the purpose of cross-examination and aim for specific results by planning his cross-examination to accomplish one or more of those purposes.

Presented here have been the considerations and methods of procedure that are available to every practitioner. Less has been said of the arts of putting these into practice. That depends to so great an extent upon the early education and the physical and mental attributes of the individual advocate that general rules cannot readily be formulated.

Training and education are helpful, but they should be so complete that no suspicion of acting can arise. Training and practice in debating are also helpful, since ability to think and to express extemporaneous thoughts clearly are prerequisites to success in the hearing room. An imposing presence, a winning personality, and a pleasing and powerful voice are also valuable assets. More important than any of these, though, are a retentive memory that enables one to carry a witness's story in mind and a mental alertness to the significance of every phrase.

The sine qua non for success in the field is unflagging industry, in advance and throughout the trial, to obtain mastery of every feature and development of the case. Without this, even a man with outstanding faculties and most thorough training will fail.

Appendix:
Other Arbitral Arenas

Duty of Fair Representation

The majority of today's labor agreements contain elaborate provisions for union security, with the most prevalent clause being a "union shop" arrangement. Under such a clause, all employees must obtain and maintain membership in the union as a condition of continued employment. Presuming the agreement contains instead a type of union security clause allowing employees the option of joining or refraining from joining the union, some employees may choose the latter. However, irrespective of the union's preference in such a case, *it has an obligation to represent all employees* in the bargaining unit for the purpose of collective bargaining over wages, hours, and other terms and conditions of employment—whether the employees are members of the union or not. Despite such a legal requirement, typically the union may give discriminatory representation, particularly regarding those employees who are hard-core holdouts.

The courts have held that unions must be accorded broad discretion in handling individual grievances. But they are not entitled to absolute immunity. *They do owe a duty of fair representation.* And a union can become liable in damages for breaching this duty.

The duties owed by unions to employees in handling grievances are more fully examined by Houselowe in "Individual Rights in Collective Labor Relations."[1] It is arguable that, whatever the needs for flexibility and wide discretion in the negotiation of new or modification of existing collective contracts, no such flexibility is either needed or appropriate when rights under a contract are involved. The standards for judgment in this area have been less than perfectly formulated. In general terms they are frequently stated as follows: The union's conduct must not be willful, arbitrary, capricious, or discriminatory. The union must not have declined to press the grievance out of laziness or prejudice, or out of unwillingness to expend money on behalf of non-members. Its decisions with respect to individual grievances must have been honest and reasonable.

The rejection of a grievance by the union must have been on the merits, in the exercise of honest discretion and/or sound judgment, following a complete and fair investigation. The rejection must not have been unjust in any respect. There must not have been bad faith or fraud. The bargaining agent must not have acted in a negligent manner.

In any event, the foreman's approach to the handling and resolution of grievances involving nonmember employees whose claims may be mishandled by the union should be no different than that accorded the member employee. He must still use the labor agreement as the *only* basis for judging the issue and applying any remedy.

In handling the grievances of nonmembers, the supervisor should be aware of two particular provisions of the Labor Management Relations Act with regard to the rights of employees. In section 7 of the Act:

> Employees shall have the right to self-organization, to form, join, or assist labor organizations, to bargain collectively through representatives of their own choosing, and to engage in other concerted activities for the purpose of collective bargaining or other mutual aid or protection, and shall also have the right to refrain from any or all of such activities except to the extent that such right may be affected by an agreement requiring membership in a labor organization as a condition of employment as authorized in section 8 (s) (3).

The second provision of the Act that comes into play most often under this type of union security clause is section 9(a):

Representatives, designated or selected for the purposes of collective bargaining by the majority of the
employees in a unit appropriate for such purposes,
shall be the exclusive representatives for all employees
in such unit for the purposes of collective bargaining in
respect to rates of pay, wages, hours of employment, or
other conditions of employment: provided, that any
individual employee or a group of employees shall
have the right at any time to present grievances to
their employer and to have such grievances adjusted,
without the intervention of the bargaining representative, as long as the adjustment is not inconsistent with
the terms of a collective bargaining contract or agreement then in effect: provided further, that the bargaining representative has been given opportunity to be
present at such adjustment.

The grievance process must be afforded to nonmembers as
well as union members and on the same terms and conditions. Any grievance should be viewed in the light of the
basic standards established by the terms of the contract
between the company and the union. All grievances, including those from nonmembers, must be limited to problems
within the scope of this standard. Any relief or remedy
applied must not violate or undermine this basic standard.

Under the management right clause, the company has
retained the right to manage and direct the working forces.
In so doing, its representatives must necessarily converse
and discuss with employees, issue them instructions and
orders, ask them questions, give them information. It *may
not "bargain" with them individually* regarding their
wages, hours, working conditions, and so on. It may *not*
endeavor to *enter into individual "agreements"* with them
covering such subjects.

The duty of fair representation has been interpreted in
various ways by the courts, and these interpretations indicate that the problems involved are as numerous as the
possible solutions to these problems. The problems arise
generally as a result of vagaries in the law and in collective

bargaining agreements, but labor experts are at odds as to
how to remedy the problems.

The duty of fair representation can be traced to its
origin in The Railway Labor Act and the landmark decision
of *Vaca* v. *Sipes* (US SUPCT, 1967, LRRM 2369) which
established the standard of "arbitrariness" to determine
whether a union has breached its duty to its members. But
the use of the standard is a "traumatic experience" because
it is difficult to apply in a legal context. An equitable accommodation of rights is needed to strike the balance between
the employee's right to press his grievance, the union's
contractual obligations to the employer and its statutory
obligations to the employee, and the employer's sometimes
conflicting obligations to both the employee and the union.

In fair representation cases, employees have the option
to pursue the employer and the union through the contract
and through the courts. Because of this grant to individuals
of a variety of methods to pursue victims to proceed against,
corrective action in this area is long overdue.

In judicial proceedings, juries have "usurped the arbitrator's role." Unions have been held liable for breach of the
duty of fair representation without a showing of breach of
the contract and without any arbitration award against the
employer. What is needed is an "allocation statement" by
the Supreme Court on the burden of proof of the parties'
competing interests.

The problems involved in fair representation cases
could be alleviated to a degree by "lawyer-free" enforcement
of the bargaining agreement. Swift and nonlegal contract
administration would be superior to the current protracted
arbitration and litigation proceedings.

Varying Standards

Since the Supreme Court's holding in Vaca v. Sipes, decisions in fair representation cases have been getting "screwier and screwier." There are varying standards for determining breach of this duty, including "negligence," "arbitrary and capricious," "bad faith," and "invidious," all

used by the courts in what amounts to a "case-by-case determination."

Although the Supreme Court has determined that Joint Area Committees (JACs) within the Teamster's jurisdiction are arbitration boards, the JACs must be "circumscribed" to protect the rights of individual employees in arbitration proceedings. With regard to any legislative proposals to define the parameters of the duty of fair representation, eventually such a proposal would end up as an amendment to the Taft-Hartley Act. The "cleansing effect" of the duty of fair representation on unions and employers still exists, and a "decent job" of meeting that duty by unions and employers is going to the ultimate benefit of employees.

Problems have arisen in this area due to "conceptual difficulties" of the law. *Vaca* v. *Sipes* made a distinction between the union's breach as a tort and the employee's right to press his grievance under the bargaining agreement. Recent decisions indicate that a union may be held liable for breaching its duty to an employee, even though the employee was discharged for cause within the meaning of the bargaining agreement, if the union fails to fully address the employee's grievance.

Although an employee may pursue his grievance in arbitration or in court, in fact the issue is one of remedies, not of forums. In an arbitration proceeding under the agreement, an arbitration is limited to "make whole" remedies, whereas in court an employee may be awarded traditional remedies including damages.

An amendment to the Taft-Hartley Act would result from efforts to define this area of law, but a finding of breach of the bargaining agreement should be based only on determination that the breach "seriously undermines the arbitral process."

Developments in Arbitration

Expediting the Arbitration Process

In limited situations, particularly where there is a large accumulation of grievances, the parties may wish to expedite arbitration procedures to their mutual satisfaction and benefit.

For example, an expedited procedure was adopted by one union and employer to cut the costs and time involved in arbitrating a backlog of grievances. Under the expedited procedure: (1) each party prepares a written statement of the grievance and facts and submits a copy to the other party; (2) each party states its thinking as to how the facts fit the contract, again with a copy to the other party; (3) both parties seek to arrive at a joint statement, but, failing that, their diverse views are submitted to the arbitrator; and (4) the arbitrator holds a hearing where he asks questions and listens to statements limited to facts and opinions submitted in the aforementioned statements. *No posthearing briefs are filed and no opinion accompanies the award* unless the arbitrator feels that comments are needed (an award without an opinion would not serve as a precedent under their plan but could be used "as a basis for conversation").

The following possibilities for expediting arbitration proceedings should be considered:

1. Dry run arbitration;
2. Prehearing statements;
3. Avoidance of "brinkmanship" prior to actual arbitration;
4. Greater use of submission agreements;
5. More effective use of factual stipulations and consequent reduced use of witnesses;
6. Elimination of transcripts, except under special circumstances;
7. Elimination of posthearing briefs;
8. Drastic shortening of opinions;
9. Early issuance of award with brief statement of reasoning, followed later by full opinion;
10. Greater use of memorandum opinions or even the equivalent of bench rulings;
11. Increased use of "instant" arbitration;

12. Expanded use of the hearing officer technique for routine cases under guidance of senior arbitrators.

One or more of the above possibilities may have real utility in a particular case. Judgment obviously must be exercised by the parties and their arbitrator in determining which, if any, of the possibilities are desirable and of beneficial promise for the given parties or for the given case.

Examples of Expedited Procedures

Limited time-strictures on the arbitrator are unusual, but many industries these days are "expediting" their arbitration procedures.

Steel

The procedure devised by the United Steelworkers and U.S. Steel is an example. Here members of special panels of arbitrators... and not the umpire... hear the so-called "one-shot" grievances. The decisions are short, and, the parties agree, cannot be used as precedent.

Brewery

A novel system was developed by the Teamsters and Anheuser Busch Brewery Company. Until about two years ago, unresolved grievances were submitted to a multiplant grievance committee consisting of company and union appointees. But this committee often deadlocked, and the time required to process grievances to arbitration was unsatisfactory. The union and its members demanded a more responsive approach.

Following a four-month strike over contractual issues, the parties redesigned the grievance and arbitration procedure so that no dispute would take more than two months to resolve. They placed a permanent neutral on the multiplant grievance committee (which now became a five-member body), and they arranged for monthly meetings of this committee so that there would be no delay at the final stage.

The new approach works in this way:

1. The committee "rides the circuit," meeting in a different city each month.

2. Before a case is appealed to the committee, the local parties stipulate all the facts, both those agreed-on and in dispute; and they secure affidavits to support their respective versions of the disputed facts.

3. They then present their fact stipulations, affidavits, and arguments to the committee. Witnesses are rarely present.

4. The committee goes into executive session. If the company and union members disagree on the disposition, the neutral casts the deciding vote and prepares a brief opinion to explain it.

In this manner, 20 to 30 cases are disposed of in two or three days.

The neutral member finds himself playing many roles. He is an arbitrator when his vote resolves the deadlock, but in other cases he may serve as a consultant, mediator, or sounding board.

One of the reasons for the frequent meetings and immediate decisions is the "status quo" provision in the new agreement. Management cannot carry out most disciplinary actions and some subcontracting, if protested, unless the committee has heard the dispute and resolved it in management's favor.

This system contains a built-in danger: When the arbitration forum becomes so accessible and the process so speedy, the local parties may not bother to try to settle their differences. It is easier to let the committee provide a quick answer. A new creative effort may therefore be required to prevent the erosion of responsibility at the local level.

Fabricating

A unique procedure is used by Allis Chalmers and the Machinists Union at some Pennsylvania plants. The parties obtain dates from the arbitrator. When a date is agreed upon, they send him written briefs which he studies on the specified date and then renders a short decision without opinion. He may, however, ask for a hearing. This procedure is used only when there is no dispute about the facts.

Airlines

Some employers and unions in the airline industry have also traveled the expedited route. This industry is characterized by tripartite system boards of adjustment. It is also known for unique grievances. Let me share one such with you.

An airline passenger agent at St. Louis, with time on his hands, decided to perfect his skills on the computer keyboard at the ticket counter. He typed out: "Now is the time for all good men to go f... themselves." As he typed, the words appeared on that little green computer screen above the keyboard. Then, along came a buddy who looked at the screen, leaned over, and pushed the button marked "Enter." By this action he conveyed the message to the computer. Seconds later, in a printout at company headquarters, there appeared this most unusual directive from St. Louis. The passenger agent was disciplined. An arbitration ensued.

Well, the arbitrator listened with a straight face. He heard a witness explain that words and phrases can be removed from the computer's memory only by using predetermined symbols, but there is no known key for the passenger agent's magic phrase. Thus, at any time, at any station or ticket office, someone may accidentally clue the computer in, and there will appear on a small green screen, "Now is the time for all good men to . . ."

It should also be known that arbitrators occasionally turn the tables. One such instance occurred during a hearing concerned with the propriety of a rule banning male flight attendants from wearing beards. The arbitrator, as fortune would have it, was one of our attractive nonmale colleagues. As part of its case, the union brought in a dozen or so neatly bearded, currently employed airline employees from various classifications to show how unreasonable the rule was. After the men, one more handsome than the man who had preceded him, had been paraded before the arbitrator, she announced demurely: "I'm not sure whether these gentlemen are witnesses or exhibits. But you should know, if they are the latter, that it has always been my practice to take exhibits home to study at my leisure!"

But back to "expedition."

Eastern Air Lines and the Machinists Union have created what they call a "time controlled" procedure. There are no transcripts or written briefs. Each side has one hour in which to present its case and must include, within the hour, its opening and closing arguments, direct examination of its own witnesses, and cross-examination of the opposing party's witnesses.

Broadcasting

In what must be one of the earliest expedited procedures, the National Association of Broadcast Engineers and Technicians and the National Broadcasting Company agreed, in 1959, that the parties could request arbitration of certain disputes within 48 hours of an occurrence, and the arbitrator was to hear the case within 72 hours thereafter and to render an award within 48 hours after the close of the hearing.

The procedure worked well, but grievances began to accumulate at an unusual rate. The umpire then suggested what came to be called "meditration." Under this procedure, the parties selected a series of grievances, summarized the facts and their positions on each case, and presented the material to the umpire, who attempted to settle them through mediation. If mediation failed, he decided the issues immediately, based on the information contained in the written statements and arguments.

A new provision in the 1967 agreement permitted either party to file a grievance directly with the umpire, who had to commence his hearings not more than 24 hours later. The umpire had to render his award no later than 24 hours after the close of the hearing, but he could send his opinion later. In this unusual industry, where time is of the essence and the show must go on, the umpire was given authority to provide injunctive or any other appropriate relief.

It became apparent to the umpire, after a while, that considerable time was spent at the hearings in discussions which would normally take place at the first step of the grievance procedure. At his suggestion, a preliminary step was established to provide for an ad hoc exchange between the parties before they appeared at the arbitration hearing.

By 1976, the office of the umpire was flooded with requests for expedited arbitrations, and NBC and NABET sought to stem the tide. In their 1976 Master Agreement they established a combination of local umpires and a national umpire, and they confined the expedited procedure to complaints concerning actions not yet effectuated. It is utilized now only when time does not permit the processing of a grievance in the regular procedure. But the parties have also underscored their intention to permit changes in operations to take effect pending the outcome of an arbitration.

In the first year of its operation, the system has reportedly worked fairly well, reducing the number of grievances submitted under the expedited procedure and heard by the national umpire, and permitting more availability for the "emergency" cases. The preliminary interchange has also helped to reduce the number of disputes submitted for arbitration.

Federal Grievance Arbitration

The Congress stumbled badly in its efforts to provide the federal sector with the first statutory grievance arbitration system in history.

The congressional purpose in writing this section of the 1978 Civil Service Reform Act was to produce a reasonably accurate facsimile of the private section grievance system complete with final and binding arbitration.

However, Congress produced a somewhat different animal. Among other problems, the resultant system is anything but final and binding in its effects.

The practical effect of the badly designed procedure will be widespread confusion, many lengthy delays, and the likely impairment, rather than improvement, of management-employee relations according to many arbitrators. It is readily apparent that arbitration in the federal sector is intended to reflect the traditional model of arbitration as practiced for many years in the unionized side of private business and industry.

However, congressional drafters wound up rather wide of the mark. Instead of a relatively simple arbitration system for helping to reduce employer-employee tensions, Congress dished up a labyrinth that almost appears to mock law as a tool of governance.

Instead of focusing on the final aspects of arbitration as the cornerstone of the policy, Congress has treated arbitration as a mere prelude to an elaborate panoply of appeals and advisory mechanisms.

The very nature of grievance arbitration is changed and its effectiveness is diminished by such an approach. As a sample of the problem, there are eight different points in the statutory plan for arbitrating grievances involving discrimination where the aggrieved employee has an opportunity to move the matter to the federal court.

By contrast with the private sector scheme where the appealing of arbitral decisions is a rarity and where such appeals often involve limited judicial review, the 1978 law provides extensive appeal procedures. In some of these, the courts are directed to conduct brand-new trials on the issues in the case.

Also deplored is the congressional failure to banish the General Accounting Office from the federal arbitration scene. Under the pre-1978 Executive Order on grievances in the federal service, the GAO had been widely criticized for playing "a bull-in-the-china shop" role in the arbitration process. Despite a 1978 congressional effort to indicate that such interference must cease, GAO's incursions into the handling of those cases have persisted. A revised statute should "finally and fully eliminate the GAO from a role in these proceedings."

If fraud is alleged, already existing criminal processes should be used. GAO has "grudgingly" recognized that the 1978 law authorized arbitrators to order back pay to remedy improper discharges and other disciplines. But meanwhile, the GAO continues to intervene in other ways in these cases. By the continued demonstration of its historic antipathy to arbitration and by its tradition to interference, the GAO "will continue to thwart" the policy goals of reducing employee-employer tensions. It appears that the only surcease for the federal system will be a flat and full congressional ban on such interventions.

Congress will have a very difficult and delicate task "to untie the complications" of the arbitration sections of the 1978 law. Nevertheless, it is possible to amend the statute to produce a process that is more of "the traditional model of (private) arbitration" than the present law.

This traditional process has been successful in "resolving commercial disputes for the last four centuries, and labor disputes for at least the last two generations."[2]

The basic function of the grievance procedure and arbitration in private employment is to assure compliance with the collective bargaining agreement. While this is also a key function of the grievance procedure and arbitration in the federal sector, another is to review or police compliance with controlling laws, rules, and regulations by federal agency employers and employees alike.

The dual role of the grievance procedure and arbitration probably was a principal factor in the congressional decision (1) to specify that each collective agreement in the federal sector "shall" provide a grievance procedure with arbitration, (2) to specify that all grievances "shall" be subject to the grievance and arbitration procedures except those specifically excluded by the collective agreement or statute, and (3) to define the term "grievance" very broadly.

Arbitral disposition of federal-sector grievances will often be governed or materially affected by laws, rules, and regulations apart from the collective agreement; another highly significant factor is that important areas of unilateral management control in the federal sector exist by statute. For some matters in the federal sector, the collective agreement and custom cannot be made the controlling "law of the plant."

Turning now to the detailed language of the statutes, it

is noted first that it is required by statute that each collective bargaining agreement in the federal sector "shall provide procedures for the settlement of grievances, including questions of arbitrability." The statute also requires that each agreement "shall . . . provide that any grievance not satisfactorily settled under the negotiated grievance procedure shall be subject to binding arbitration which may be invoked by either" the union or the federal agency employer.

The same statute provides, with only two exceptions, that the contractual grievance procedure and arbitration (since the grievance procedure must provide for arbitration) "shall be the exclusive procedures for resolving grievances which fall within its coverage." The two exceptions involve certain subjects or issues for which employees are given the option of using either (but not both) the contractual grievance and arbitration procedures or certain purely statutory procedures.

The rule concerning "coverage" of the contractual grievance procedure is simple. All grievances are automatically covered by the grievance procedure and can go to arbitration unless excluded by agreement of the parties or unless specifically excluded by statute. Regarding exclusions the statute provides in substance for the following:

1. Any collective bargaining agreement may exclude any matter from the application of the agreement's grievance procedure.
2. Grievances concerning the following subjects or issues are specifically excluded from the grievance procedure and arbitration: (1) political activities; (2) retirement, life insurance, or health insurance; (3) suspension or removal for national security; (4) examination, certification, or appointment; (5) classification of any position if the classification does not result in the reduction in grade or pay of an employee.

What can qualify as a "grievance" in federal employment? The term "grievance" is defined very broadly as follows:

"Grievance" means any complaint—

1. by any employee concerning any matter relating to the employment of the employee;
2. by any labor organization concerning any matter relating to the employment of any employee; or
3. by any employee, labor organization, or agency concerning the effect or interpretation, or a claim of breach, of a collective bargaining agreement; or any claimed violation, misinterpretation, or misapplication of any law, rule, or regulation affecting conditions of employment."

Thus, to reiterate, it is clear (1) that every collective agreement in the federal sector must provide a grievance procedure and arbitration, (2) that the door to the grievance procedure and arbitration is open wide to all grievances except those specifically excluded by the agreement or statute, and (3) that the term "grievance" is defined broadly with the result that an extremely wide variety of complaints will qualify for access to the grievance procedure and arbitration.

Interest Arbitration and Collective Bargaining

Interest arbitration is the procedure whereby an arbitrator fills out the terms of the settlement on all the issues that the parties could not resolve themselves. The arbitrator takes on the issues on which the parties reached an impasse, and offers his binding version of how they would have resolved those issues. This kind of arbitration is to be distinguished from grievance arbitration where the award is limited much more sharply in its scope. The typical grievance award will deal with an individual grievant's complaint that he was discharged, laid off, or otherwise deprived of benefits or the opportunity to work, in violation of the existing management-union contract.

Almost a decade of experience under New York City's

Interest Arbitration Statute reveals that "there has clearly been no chilling of the bargaining process" caused by the availability of arbitration as an alternate process, according to Arvid Anderson, the chairman of New York City's Office of Collective Bargaining.

Despite the classic apprehension about making arbitration the stand-in for bargaining, the New York City record presents a quite different perception of reality. As Anderson put it in his speech to a May 5, 1981, session of the National Academy of Arbitrators Annual Meeting in Maui, Hawaii:

> "Contrary to predictions, there has been a very low utilization rate; only 8.6 percent of all contract disputes have required the use of impasse procedures. And more than half of that number represent awards which were the confirmation, in whole or in part, of the bargaining process of the parties."[3]

New York City's chief mediator also pointed to the near-absence of strikes under the interest arbitration law approved by the New York City Council in 1972. It became a part of the state's labor relations statutes for the public sector.

Since the enactment of the New York City law, there have been only three strikes over new contract terms. Nearly 600 individual contracts were negotiated during this period. There was a five-and-one-half hour firefighter strike in 1973 which was settled by arbitration, a ten-day strike of off-track betting clerks in 1979 and a one-week strike of interns and residents in 1981 submitted to binding arbitration.

In offering this favorable report card, Anderson also noted that collective bargaining—not interest arbitration— has been the prime process for setting the basic wage and benefit patterns in New York.

Interest arbitrations have concerned disputes where attempts were made to increase the basic wage pattern of the city or have involved special conditions of employment, such as whether or not one-man supervisory patrols should be implemented in the police department, or what the proper rate of compensation should be for two-man sanitation crews assigned to do the work previously performed by three-man crews.

Special stress must be given to the part of the record indicating that the interest arbitration awards have not exceeded the size of the negotiated settlements during the same period.

The board has had to reduce an impasse panel's award in only two cases in nine years.

As mentioned, there were only two cases during the nearly ten-year period where the awards were found to be inconsistent with negotiated settlements. In the appellate process, these awards were reduced by the unanimous decisions of the tripartite board of collective bargaining to conform the awards to the city's basic wage patterns. It is also significant that less than one-fourth of all impasse panel awards have been appealed to the board of collective bargaining and that no awards have been successfully appealed to the courts.

Arbitration and Supreme Court Rulings

Three decisions handed down by the U.S. Supreme Court should spur employers and unions to draft specific contract language to protect against wildcat strikes, against individual litigation based upon statutory rights, and against charges of failure to represent.

The three rulings are Complete Auto Transit, Inc., v. Reis (107 LRRM 2145) holding that an employer may not collect damages against individual workers who violate a no-strike agreement by carrying out an unauthorized wildcat strike; Barrentine v. Arkansas-Best Freight System (24 WH cases 1284) allowing an employee to bring court action under the Fair Labor Standards Act even after denial of his grievance; and Clayton v. UAW and ITT Gilfillan (107 LRRM 2385) holding that a worker whose grievance is rejected does not have to exhaust the union's internal appeals before suing both the union and employer.

Each of these decisions weakens some aspect of collective bargaining.

In all three cases litigation in the federal courts was preferred over the machinery selected by the union and the employer for settling their disputes. Justices Brennan, White, Marshall, Blackmun, and Stevens were in the majority on each occasion. The dissenting justices—Chief Justice Burger and Justice Rehnquist, sometimes joined by Justices Powell and Stewart—"pointed out the increasing pressure on the courts and the national policy in favor of contract grievance procedures as a preferred method for settling disputes."

Remedies for Wildcats

Turning to the specific cases, the remedies an employer has to deal with wildcat strikes are "illusory." Discharge is "seldom realistic," and wholesale discharges are impractical while selective discharges may be illegal. Injunctions against striking workers are generally prohibited, unions seldom discipline their striking workers, and employer suits for damages against unions are unlikely to succeed.

To remedy this problem, it is suggested the parties add new language to their grievance procedures. "For example, a specific reference to possible noncompliance by union members with the union's no-strike commitment may make a wildcat strike an arbitrable issue subject to injunction, damages and discharge sanctions."

Issues such as the minimum wage claim under Barrentine could be resolved by broadening an impartial arbitrator's authority to determine certain statutory questions plus an administrative practice of obtaining a grievant's written consent to having such matters submitted to arbitration. An arbitrator's power also could be expanded to include the broad range of relief that may be contained in the statute, sometimes including the right to award actual and liquidated damages, reasonable attorney's fees and costs.

The joint grievance committee system of arbitration found in Teamster contracts "is so clearly defective as an impartial mechanism that it is not surprising that we keep seeing it tested in the courts in cases such as Barrentine. I continue to be astonished that the Supreme Court refers to this system as 'arbitration'."

Grievance and arbitration procedures could incorporate a reference to an internal procedure by providing that the time limitation for filing a grievance for arbitration shall be tolled if a grievant makes use of available union procedures to seek review of a union decision not to proceed with the grievance. Unions concerned about "failure to represent" litigation could provide for impartial review and authorize an impartial tribunal to reactivate a grievance and send it to an arbitrator who would be authorized to grant the complete relief available by litigation.

If such changes in contract language were adopted at the bargaining table, the parties would be able to "respond to recent cases and to protect against a substantial amount of unnecessary litigation between union members and the contractual parties."

Other Issues

The balance between a union's desire for access to information and an employee's concern about disclosure is a "classic conflict between individual and group interests." An employer's refusal to give employee test scores to a union without the employees' consent was upheld by the Supreme Court in Detroit Edison Company v. NLRB (100 LRRM 2728), and a firm's refusal to give a union the names of employees with lung disease without the consent of those employees was approved by the board in Johns Manville Sales Corporation and Chemical Workers. (105 LRRM 1379).

The balance between an employee's desire not to disclose information and the employer's desire to obtain information necessary for decisions often involves the controversial issue of truth verification with such methods as polygraph and voice stress.

The balance between employee access and an employer's desire to maintain confidentiality is tested when employees seek to correct historical data or to gain access to tests. The final issue involves the balance between the protection of personal privacy and government regulations and control of private information systems.

Arbitrators are reluctant to rely on polygraphs as evidence that employees are lying but will use such evidence as proof of innocence. Awards involving an employee's refusal to take a polygraph are "unclear and mixed." However, "the weight of arbitral authority appears to uphold discharge for employees who refuse" to submit to searches. This illustrates that arbitrators distinguish between "intellectual and physical privacy" and feel that intellectual privacy is entitled to greater protection.

Finality

While arbitral awards traditionally have been deemed final and binding, there have emerged two lines of cases that are exceptions. One involves the impact of external law such as the FLSA claim under Barrentine or the discrimination allegation under Alexander v. Gardner-Denver. (7 FEP Cases 81).

Finality in arbitration is now "a much more tenuous concept" which is "going through a process of evolution" but the procedure will be strengthened with passage of time. To those who wonder whether to use arbitration when there is a possibility that a grievant also will seek to litigate, the answer clearly is yes. In the vast majority of cases arbitration will provide an end to the dispute; the handful of cases that go on to litigation are difficult to win.

CITATIONS

1. Bureau of National Affairs (BNA), Washington, D.C. 10007.
2. BNA. See *Labor Relations Reporter,* Sept. 1981.
3. BNA. See *Annual Proceedings of the National Academy of Arbitrators,* 1981.

Bibliography

A Selected Bibliography

Aaron, Benjamin *et al, The Future of Labor Arbitration in America* (New York: American Arbitration Association, 1976).

Aaron, Benjamin, *The Impact of Public Employment Grievance Settlement on the Labor Arbitration Process* (Los Angeles: University of California, Institute of Industrial Relations, 1976).

Association of the Bar of the City of New York, *An Outline of Arbitration Procedure* (New York: 1956).

Baderschneider, Earl R. and Miller, Paul F. (editors), *Labor Arbitration in Health Care: A Case Book* (New York: Spectrum Publications, Inc., 1976).

Baer, Walter E., *The Operating Managers Labor Relations Guidebook* (Dubuque, Iowa: Kendall-Hunt Pub. Co., 1980).

Baer, Walter E., *Discipline and Discharge Under the Labor Agreement* (New York: American Management Association, 1972).

Baer, Walter E., *The Labor Arbitration Guide* (Homewood: Dow Jones-Irwin, 1974).

Bernstein, Merton C., *Private Dispute Settlement* (New York: Free Press, 1978).

Bureau of National Affairs, Editorial Staff. *Grievance Guide* (Washington: The Bureau of National Affairs, Inc., Fifth Edition, 1978).

California, University of. Institute of Industrial Relations. *Preparing and Presenting Arbitration Cases;* Selected Addresses from the 1954 Conference on Arbitration and Labor Relations (Berkeley: 1954).

Coulson, Robert, *Labor Arbitration: What You Need to Know* (New York: American Arbitration Association, 1973).

Davey, Harold W., *Improving Grievance Arbitration: The Practitioners Spear,* Iowa State Univ., Industrial Relations Center, Ames, Iowa.

Elkin, Randyl and Hewitt, Thomas L., *Successful Arbitration: An Experiential Approach* (Reston: Reston Publishing Company, Inc., 1980).

Elkouri, Frank and Edna Asper Elkouri, *How Arbitration Works,* 3rd ed., (Washington: Bureau of National Affairs, Third Edition, 1973).

Fairweather, Owen, *Practice and Procedure in Labor Arbitration* (Washington: Bureau of National Affairs, 1973).

Fleming, R. W., *The Labor Arbitration Process* (Urbana: University of Illinois Press, 1965).

Harrison, Allan J., *Preparing and Presenting Your Arbitration Case* (Washington: The Bureau of National Affairs, Inc., 1979).

Hill, Marvin, J. R., and Sinicropi, Anthony V., *Evidence in Arbitration* (Washington: The Bureau of National Affairs, Inc., 1980).

————, *Remedies in Arbitration* (Washington: The Bureau of National Affairs, Inc., 1981).

Kagel, Sam, *Anatomy of a Labor Arbitration* (Washington: Bureau of National Affairs, 1961).

Kochan, Thomas A. *et al, Dispute Resolution Under Fact-Finding and Arbitration: An Empirical Analysis* (New York: American Arbitration Association, 1979).

Landis, Brook, *Value Judgments in Arbitration: A Case Study of Saul Wallen* (Ithaca: Cornell University, New York State School of Industrial and Labor Relations, 1977).

Lapp, John A., *Labor Arbitration, Principles and Procedures* (New York: National Foremen's Institute, 1946).

Loewenberg, J. Joseph *et al, Compulsory Arbitration: An*

International Comparison (Lexington, MA: D. C. Heath and Company, 1976).

McKelvey, Jean T. (editor), *The Duty of Fair Representation* (Ithaca: NYSSILR, 1977).

National Academy of Arbitrators, *Proceedings of the Annual Conference on Labor Arbitration,* 1948 through Present (Washington: The Bureau of National Affairs, Inc., Annually 1948 through Present). 33 volumes through 1981.

Nolan, Dennis R., *Labor Arbitration Law and Practice in a Nut Shell* (St. Paul: West Publishing Company, 1979).

Pops, Gerald M., *Emergence of the Public Sector Arbitrator* (Lexington, Massachusetts: D. C. Heath and Company, 1976).

Prasow, Paul and Edward Peters, *Arbitration and Collective Bargaining: Conflict Resolution in Labor Relations* (New York: McGraw-Hill, 1970).

Schoen, Sterling H. and Hilgert, Raymond L., *Cases in Collective Bargaining and Industrial Relations: A Decisional Approach* (Homewood: Richard D. Irwin, Inc., Third Edition, 1978).

Scheinman, Martin F., *Evidence and Proof in Arbitration* (Ithaca: NYSSILR, 1977).

Seide, Katharine, *A Dictionary of Arbitration* (Dobbs Ferry, New York: Oceana Publications, Inc., 1970).

Slegel, Boaz, *Proving Your Arbitration Case* (Washington: Bureau of National Affairs, 1961).

Spitz, John A., (Ed.), *Employee Discipline* (Institute of Industrial Relations, University of California, Los Angeles: 1977).

Stern, James L. *et al, Final-Offer Arbitration: The Effects on Public Safety Employee Bargaining* (Lexington, MA: D. C. Heath and Company, 1975).

Stone, Morris and Baderschneider, Earl R., *Arbitration of Discrimination Grievances: A Case Book* (New York: American Arbitration Association, 1974).

Teple, Edwin R. and Moberly, Robert B., *Arbitration and Conflict Resolution* (Unit Six of Labor Relations and Social Problems) (Washington: The Bureau of National Affairs, Inc., 1979).

Tracy, Estelle R. (Editor), *Arbitration Cases in Public Employment* (New York: American Arbitration Association, 1969).

Trotta, Maurice S., *Arbitration of Labor-Management Disputes* (New York: AMACOM, 1974).

Updegraff, Clarence M., *Arbitration and Labor Relations* (Washington: Bureau of National Affairs, 3rd Edition, 1970).

U.S. Department of Labor, Bureau of Labor Statistics. *Grievance and Arbitration Procedures in State and Local Agreements* (Washington, D.C.: U.S. Government Printing Office, 1974).

Zack, Arnold M. and Bloch, Richard I., *The Arbitration of Discipline Cases: Concepts and Questions* (New York: American Arbitration Association, 1979).

Zack, Arnold, *Understanding Grievance Arbitration in the Public Sector* (Washington, D.C.: U.S. Government Printing Office, 1974).

Arbitration Awards

Bureau of National Affairs, *Labor Arbitration Reports* (Washington: The Bureau of National Affairs, Inc., Weekly Reports, Bound Volumes Published Semiannually since 1946). Cost: $353 annually (1980).

Commerce Clearing House, *Labor Arbitration Awards* (San Rafael: Commerce Clearing House, Inc., Weekly Reports, Bound Volumes Published Semiannually since 1946). Cost: $345 annually (1980) for each of two years.

Labor Relations Press, *Labor Arbitration Index* (Fort Washington, PA.: Labor Relations Press, 12 issues yearly, index published since 1970). Cost: $185 annually (1980).

Prentice Hall, *Industrial Relations Guide* (Englewood Cliffs, N.J.: Prentice Hall).

Prentice Hall, *Public Personnel Administration: Labor-Management Relations* (Englewood Cliffs, N.J.: Prentice Hall).

Index

JUN